LEADING CORPORATE CLANS

Dawn Jarvis Featuring Munu Wuthuga Dadarkiin

Published by People & OD Partners Publishing

First published in 2022

Copyright © Dawn Jarvis 2022

ISBN 978-0-645-50851-2

Illustrations by People & OD Partners Publishing
Designed by Softwood Self-Publishing

CONTENTS

ACKNOWLEDGEMENTS AND DEDICATIONS

Dedication

This book is dedicated to my husband and children, Tony, Jess, and Liam. They have supported me to start my own business, to have the time to study, learn, grow, and put the hard work in to enable me to get the experience necessary to write a book like this. Without your unstinting love, support, and cheer-leading skills, I would not be the person I am today, and I would not have written this book. I love you all, always and forever.

Acknowledgements

Firstly - to my many and varied clients who have benefited from the various versions of the STELLAR MODEL® as its evolution has occurred; to the public sector leaders in the NHS and local government in the UK and in the Australian public health systems and local government sectors; to the various, occasional private sector clients who helped me shape my business. Thank you all for unwittingly being my test subjects and for doing the hard yards of "the work" of the model as it has developed. I know all of you have benefitted in one way or another and you are all committed to the long, winding, and perpetual road that is leadership development.

Secondly - to my collaborators and partners who have shaped the STELLAR MODEL® over the years in chronological order:

John Scott - a long-standing in-house work colleague who is wise beyond words, ethical beyond reproach, and speaks the truth to any power, whatever the personal consequences. You taught me more about leadership and friend-ship than you will ever know, and you play a mean drum!

Nicola Roberts - first came to me for coaching supervision, then worked with me as a coach associate, and now trains and supervises coaches herself and has wisdom beyond mine on the genesis of the models I refer to. You are kind, supportive, and challenging in equal measure. Your research for this book has been invaluable, and without you and your beautiful, persistent nagging, I wouldn't have had the confidence or resilience to have put pen to paper. Thank you.

Diane Wilkinson – a fellow alumni of National Training Laboratories (NTL)[1], long-time collaborator, and friend. We planned so much joint delivery of our work, which was kyboshed by the pandemic in 2020, and you cajoled me to make the move to online. What fun we had, how much we learned! Without you, the model would not have shifted to the 2020 version and my Female Leadership and Growth (FLAG)[2] online movement would not have begun. Our regular Zoom discussions are fun and fierce at times as we continue to collaborate in the true sense of the word. We have been there for each other through the toughest of times, and I hope we always will.

Holly Cook – wow, what a joyful surprise meeting you in 2020. And what a weird first meeting that was! How we have developed our collaborative partnership since then and what an amazing woman you are. If only I had known as much, been as much, and done as much as you when I was your age, imagine what I could have achieved, and imagine what you will achieve in the future! You truly are the next generation of Organisational Development (OD), and I am delighted to have met you and to see you in action.

Thirdly - my People & OD Partners team. Several of those mentioned above feature in that, as do a couple of my family, who have mentions elsewhere. The standout person here is Michelle Elliott, our Operations Coordinator. Michelle has, at time of writing, been with us for less than a year and is amazing. In her twenty hours a week for us, she has turned our collateral, our content, our organisational capacity on its head, and what is certain is that, without her, I would not have had the time or the clarity to put pen to paper. Thank you for your creativity, consistency, and can-do attitude. You are a joy to work with. Thank you also to Rachael Peel, our in-house Organisational Psychologist. Her verification of the STELLAR MODEL® questionnaire and development of the Maturity Matrix (see Chapter 11) is invaluable. It is now allowing us to work towards creating "norms" for responses, to provide benchmarks and to add to the ever-growing pool of research we are creating from this tool. Thank you.

Fourthly – She Mentors[3]. This is a mentorship exchange club, whereby, as a member, I can give and receive two mentoring sessions a month (on a huge variety of subjects that I or the other women have experience in) with other women, booking from a range of around 700 women from all over Australia,

---

1   NTL Institute (2022). Organization Development. Available at: https://www.ntl.org/organizational-development/

2   FLAG Female Leadership and Growth (2022). People and OD Partners. Available at: https://peopleandodpartners.com/what-we-do-1

3   She Mentors (2022). Mentoring for Purpose-Driven Women. Available at: https://shementors.com.au/

with a huge range of skills, experiences, and specialist interests. Even in the short time I have been a member, I have had wisdom from some excellent women on the writing of this book, its structure, content, and artwork. Again, without the group, my confidence and persistence to continue would not have been boosted and remained as strong as it has. Thank you to Ali Adey, founder of She Mentors, for setting up such a vibrant and useful community and Molly Burley for making sure we all get a great experience in the community.

Fifthly – Softwood Self-Publishing[4]. Thank you to Allan Scott from Mill House Media[5] for introducing me to Softwood. Nathan, Carl, and Maddy have been supportive, kind, and effective, and working with them has given me the creative freedom that I just wasn't getting from the other various publishing deals on offer to me. They understood what I wanted from the first moment we met, and they have bags of integrity and are a joy to work with. Thank you all for your expertise, support, and what you have taught me so far. I am sure there is lots still to learn.

Finally, and very importantly, Munu Wuthuga Dardakiin[6]. How lucky I was that I met Munu. He has listened and understood my deep desire to create a respectful way to incorporate a small element of the culture that has, since the beginning of time, been ever present in Australia. I describe the STELLAR MODEL® as being connected and holistic, each element needing to be in balance so that all the elements can work together to create, develop, or improve leadership teams. From my attempts to learn more about the indigenous culture of Australia, out of a deep respect, it struck me that this culture reminded me of my view of the STELLAR MODEL®. I also knew as I was writing the book here in Australia that I wanted to incorporate some of that culture into the book. Munu understood that and what I was trying to do and very quickly saw past my model and into the story he would create through his art and his story telling. He has come up with what I think is a masterpiece, which we both hope will go some way to connecting indigenous culture and heritage with the corporate world. The corporate world might consider bringing in more of the type of wisdom that the Elders, spirits, and traditional ideas show and how that could be brought into solutions for the current issues in workplaces in Australia; wouldn't that be a great outcome!

4   SWS Softwood Self Publishing (2022). Putting you in control of your publishing journey. Available at: https://www.swspublishing.com/
5   Mill House Media (2022). Available at: https://millhousemedia.co.uk/
6   Online as @nullenart (2022). Available at: https://www.instagram.com/nullenart/?hl=en

PART ONE
INTRODUCTIONS

Our Path
to the Present

PART 1 - INTRODUCTIONS

Welcome, fabulous reader!

Welcome to this book. We are so delighted to be able to get to the point where we can compile a volume with all the work we have been doing with leaders and teams over the last few decades. When you support people to make changes to the way they work, and therefore to how their system works, and if you are any good at it (and our clients tell us we are, so we will go with that), you keep getting inundated with work to do, more clients to support, more teams to develop, and more systems to improve. Therefore, despite several previous attempts over the last ten years, this is the first time we have been able to compile our models, our collateral, our teachings in one place and spend the time to curate it into something we hope will be useful to you as a leader, as a member of a leadership team, or as a fellow supporter of that group. We hope you feel able to either read the book from cover to cover or dip in and out of the parts you need to find what you are looking for in the moment, coming back to the rest when you need it.

We are always happy to connect to like-minded, curious souls, so if you have any questions or comments or want to add anything from your own work to our thinking, please get in touch. It would be lovely to grow our network and hear how you got on using some of our tools in your team and your development.

Dawn

Dawn and People & OD Partners Team
admin@peopleandodpartners.com

CHAPTER 1

THE STELLAR MODEL®

The hero of this book is our model for leadership and team coaching, the STELLAR MODEL®.

If you Google 'leadership models', you will get around 661,000,000 results in 0.51 seconds. There are many excellent models (and some not so good), many books, and many theories about what makes successful leaders and successful leadership teams. Indeed, every now and again, up pops the debate about whether the team is a thing of the past and whether the new ways of working that we have developed over the last few years as a result of the pandemic have changed the nature of team working forever. Society, workplaces, and how we work together will continue to evolve, as it has done since we moved into settlements as humans and began to share workloads. For a long time to come, we will still need to work and engage with others in groups to get things done. Therefore, we offer you the content of this book to help make working with others in groups more effective, whether or not you call that a "team".

This book and our STELLAR MODEL® aren't intended to prove that any of the previous models are wrong or that a fully-formed team (or group) or collaborative project arrangement is the best or worst structure to get things done, or even that what we are saying here is entirely right or correct. Far from it. Much of what we are saying here may have been said before. Then you might be asking, "What's the point of coming up with a new model?" You might, of course, be right, but we will let you be the judge of that when you have read the book.

What we are trying to do here with this book and what we have success-fully been doing with teams across the globe for many years is pull together all that we know about what works in practice (to do with building, supporting, and developing high performing teams).

We will share the growth and development of the STELLAR MODEL® with you to explain how we have worked and worked it to refine it into the model we have now, how that has been honed for use with our clients, and how we have successfully been using the latest version if it for the last three years.

In this book, as you will see later in Chapter 10, we have also provided a story, a tale, a yarn, if you will, to sit behind the model, which comes from a collaboration with Munu Wuthuga Dardakiin (more about Munu later).

We know our model is a connected set of elements that all must work together in synchronicity for the system that is the leadership team to flourish. Most of this book has been written on the Gold Coast in Queensland, Australia. This is the traditional land of the Yugambeh Language People[7] and led us to know that we had to collaborate with the original people of the land on which we work. After several other attempts, we connected with Munu (originally from Cape York, now living on this land), who we forged a great collaborative partnership with around the middle of 2021. Munu painted the model and created the story of the Seven Clans.

His immediate response when he saw the model in our original graphics was that it looked to him like seven clans that formed a tribe, who needed to work together to make the tribe flourish. It was like he immediately understood what we were trying to do with teams and understood our model.

Figure 1: Dawn and Munu when they made their agreement
to work together: 29 October 2021

7   Yugambeh Language People (2022). The Yugambeh Museum Language and Heritage Research Centre. Available at: https://www.yugambeh.com/

How did we get to the STELLAR MODEL® that we have in 2022?

We have been using versions of this interconnected approach since around 2007, with teams and coaching leaders. It all started when we began supporting teams, not just by facilitating their "team-building" events in the style of a "facilitator", but by employing the tools and techniques of a "Group Process Facilitator", taking this from the organisational development approaches, with which we had been trained via the National Training Laboratories (NTL) Institute[8], led by the amazing Mee-Yan Cheung-Judge[9].

A brief diversion to explain Group Process Facilitation

You may know what we mean when we call our work "Group Process Facilitation", in which case, feel free to move to the next chapter or seek out and refresh yourself with the wonderful works of Gervase Bushe[10] and others from the NTL family.

If you don't know what we mean, it should become apparent in more detail in Chapter 7, where we cover our Organisational Development (OD) approach and the eight stages of the OD cycle. In brief, the difference between what we might call "regular facilitation" and "group process facilitation" may sometimes seem subtle, but we think it is hugely important.

Facilitating the group process is still about the task (the agenda, the timekeeping, getting the operational jobs done, and making sure the team comes out with the specific practical items they need, which they were holding the workshop for in the first place, for example a strategic plan. And it is also about maintenance of the relationships and interaction of the group.

For example, a traditional facilitator will often not pause their carefully constructed agenda to divert to picking up any underlying issues that arise between the participants at the workshop. So, if an attendee drops a bomb into the discussion by saying something like, "This always happens when we talk about this; we never get to make any real decisions", a traditional facilitator might skate over this. They might suggest it is left on a flip chart on the wall, which might have the heading on it "car park" (usually where all the things that can't be dealt with during a workshop are left) and handed back to the group's leader to deal with "out of session" when they all get back to the office.

---

8   NTL Institute (2022). Organization Development.
    Available at: https://www.ntl.org/organizational-development/

9   Cheung-Judge, M.Y. (2022). NTL Institute Overview. Available at: https://ntl-od.uk/overview

10 Bushe, G. (2022) Gervase Bushe Professional Bio.
    Available at: http://www.gervasebushe.ca/probio.htm

However, as a skilled and well-trained group process facilitator and OD practitioner, increasingly referred to as a "team coach", you will generally if contracted for, pre-agreed with the group (more on what we mean by that later) and psychologically safe to do so:

1. Notice what is going on with and between the people,

2. Name what we see,

3. Deal with what is most important to support the health and development of the group or system.

Using the example above, we might ask, "What does everyone else have to say about this?" or "Does anyone else feel like this?" or "Shall we pause for some time and talk about what has just been said?"

Figure 2 shows the main differences between task and maintenance of groups.

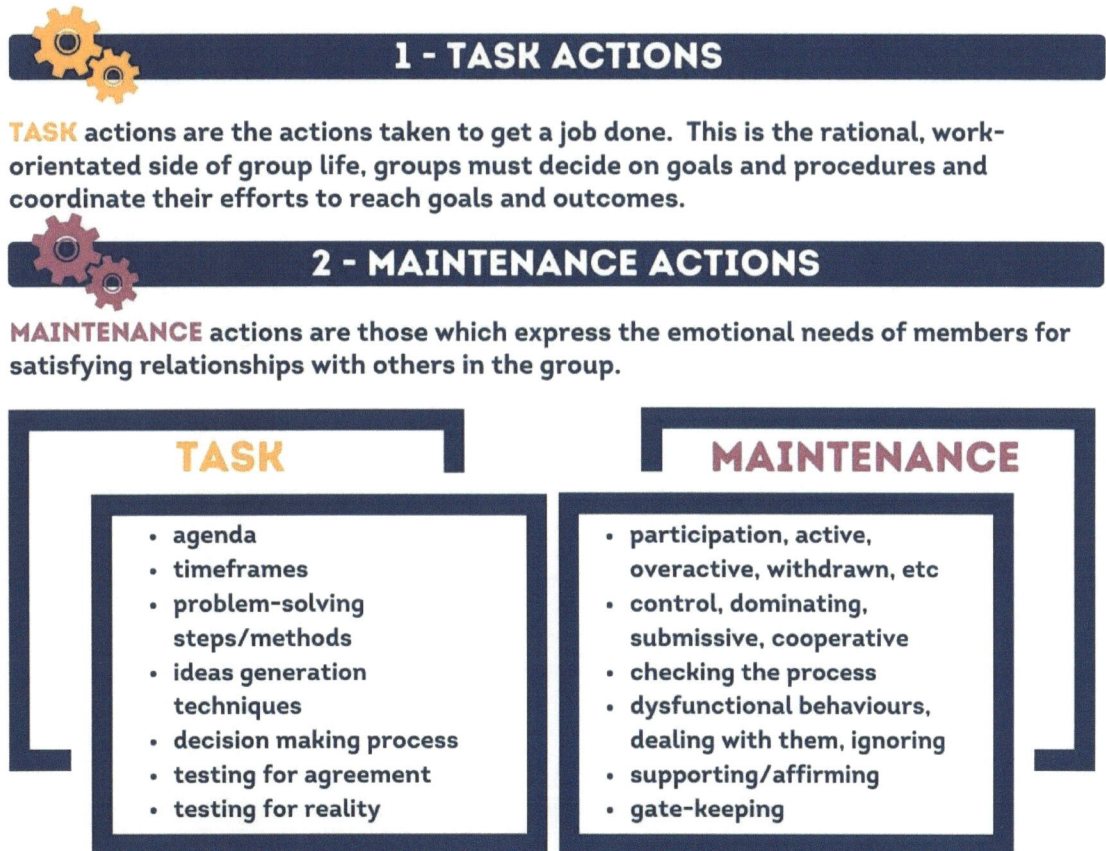

1 - TASK ACTIONS

TASK actions are the actions taken to get a job done. This is the rational, work-orientated side of group life, groups must decide on goals and procedures and coordinate their efforts to reach goals and outcomes.

2 - MAINTENANCE ACTIONS

MAINTENANCE actions are those which express the emotional needs of members for satisfying relationships with others in the group.

TASK	MAINTENANCE
• agenda • timeframes • problem-solving steps/methods • ideas generation techniques • decision making process • testing for agreement • testing for reality	• participation, active, overactive, withdrawn, etc • control, dominating, submissive, cooperative • checking the process • dysfunctional behaviours, dealing with them, ignoring • supporting/affirming • gate-keeping

Figure 2: Group Process Facilitation: Task and Maintenance, taken from the work of Brendan Reddy[11]

11 Reddy, W.B. (1994). Intervention Skills: Process Consultation for Small Groups and Teams. San Francisco: Jossey-Bass

The more we did this work, the more we searched for models already available to "hang" the kind of work we were doing onto. The model most closely aligned with our work at the time was that outlined by Patrick Lencioni: The Five Dysfunctions of a Team[12]. However, as we worked with the elements of this model, we realised it didn't quite work, for two main reasons. Firstly, there always seemed as though there was something missing, and we needed to add or modify how we used it with our clients. Secondly, we couldn't get past the uncomfortableness of the name; having dysfunction in the title started us off with a negative feeling. This might sound a bit silly, but we very much subscribe to the "trust your gut" mantra and so had to listen to those feelings.

Because we thought the name was slightly off-putting, as general advocates of the Appreciative Inquiry[13] school of thought and strength-based practice, we felt some dissonance and instinctively pulled away from something that had "dysfunctions" in the title rather than something like "how to build a functioning team". Although, to be fair, the inside of Lencioni's book is all about how to build high functioning teams.

Secondly, we found we were regularly adding a few things to the model; the five points just didn't seem to do it. Don't get the wrong impression; it was still a great book and a great model, and if every team were following it, the world of work and teams would be a better place. There should be absolutely no impression given here that Lencioni's book isn't what might be called a seminal or transformation work in the field of team dynamics and functioning. For us, it just wasn't quite the right model to build our work upon, potentially due to the needs of the main sectors in which we predominantly work.

This led us to realise that we needed to create something that we completely resonated with, which we felt we could recommend to the teams we worked with as a compass for their development journey on an ongoing basis; and who *doesn't* want to create their own leadership model!

Therefore, in 2017, we started to pull together our version of a model to collate the various ways of working with teams, and this became something called the STAR Model (see Figure 3). This had purpose and the WHY at the centre and split the WHAT of a team, the practical application of getting things done, from the HOW of a team; how they behaved to each other, how they acted around conflict, etc.

12 Lencioni, P. M. (2002) The five dysfunctions of a team. Jossey-Bass.

13 Stavros, J.M, Godwin, L.N. & Cooperrider, D.L. (2015). Organization Development and the Strengths Revolution. In: W.J. Rothwell, J. Stavros, R.L. Sullivan, Practicing Organization Development: Leading Transformation and Change. (4th ed., p. 96). New Jersey: Wiley.

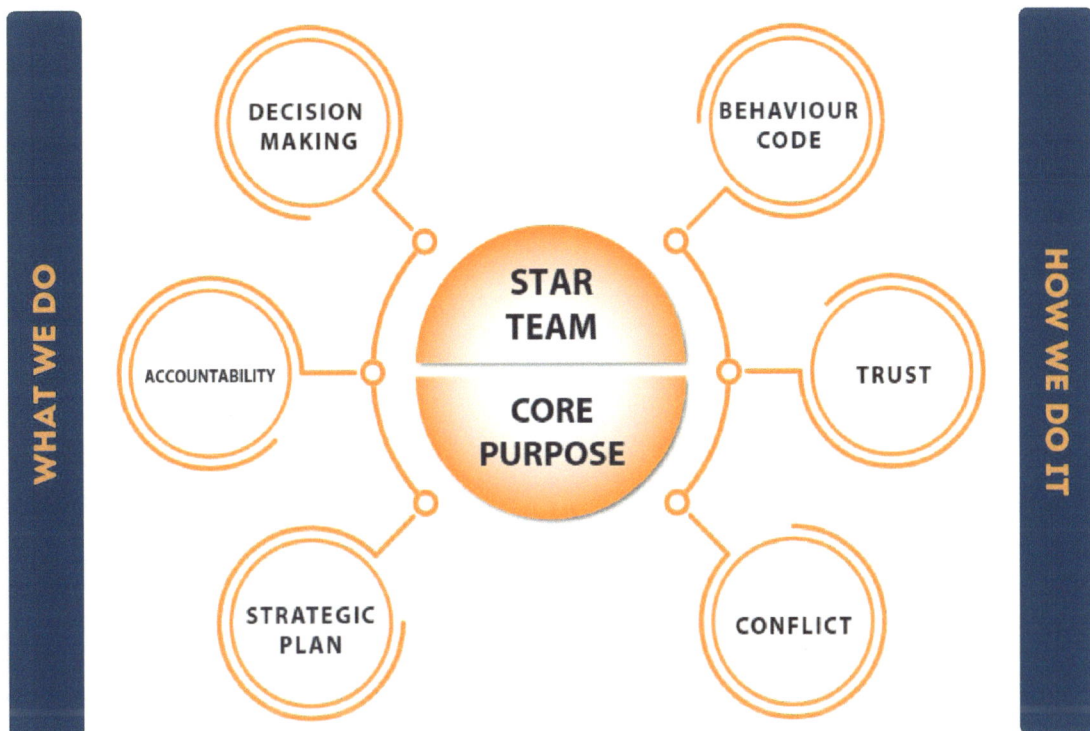

Figure 3: 2017-2019 Representation of STAR©, People & OD Partners Ltd

We worked with teams and posed a series of questions to them at the start of the engagement to get a baseline based on the elements of the model. At this stage, these were hard copy, completed in person, and collated live in a workshop, so not too successful for those attendees who might have been reflectors or where there wasn't quite the right psychological safety (more about this later) yet built (see Figure 4 over page).

Figure 4 shows the questionnaire we had at the time. We used the questions we felt we needed to have the answers to in order to support the team, so this version was what we used for a while. Since those early days, we have gone online, used various ways to gather this information prior to the event, and changed the questions as the model has evolved.

We have now reached the stage where the model and the questions have been verified by Rachael, our in-house organisational psychologist, as a robust psychometric tool, and we are amassing enough information from respondents to form our own "norm" group. This will be valuable for teams as we go forward and we will be able to let them know what most teams' responses are to any given question to help them decide the areas they would like to

Element	Assessment Question	G	A	R
Core Purpose	1. We have a clear, shared purpose that we can succinctly explain to anyone at any time and the words we use are a uniform, shared explanation of why we exist, what we do and how we do it. 2. Our wider team is clear on our core purpose, we know they could explain it to stakeholders, customers, service users and colleagues. 3. Our core purpose drives all of our decisions and creates a passionate connection to our work for our wider team.			
Behaviour Code	1. I feel valued, included and respected by this team. 2. We have a clear, agreed code of behaviour and we try to live up to it at all. When we don't, we apologise and reset. 3. We are all comfortable giving and receiving feedback from each other about our behaviour.			
Trust	1. We trust each other, completely. Meaning that I believe that everyone in this team is competent, authentic, consistent, transparent and has integrity. 2. I trust that people in this team value the delivery of team goals above personal or individual achievements. 3. I trust everyone in this team to have my back and to be honest with me when they don't agree with my views, or think I am in the wrong.			
Conflict	1. There is an openness amongst us and we encourage healthy debates to bring out a diversity of views. 2. People feel comfortable talking against the group think. 3. Problems and conflicts are not swept under the rug. The team works through them openly.			
Decision Making	1. When we make a decision we stick to it outside the room even if it wasn't our individual preferred choice, delivering the team decision with purpose. 2. We implement the decisions we make and are clear about what, when, who and how decisions are to be implemented 3. Our decisions are communicated to our wider organisation quickly and concisely and we ask for feedback about how they have been received and whether implementation has led or an improvement – we learn from our decisions.			
Accountability	1. Everyone in this team is clear what their deliverables and KPIs are and can explain them to others using the SMARTER approach. 2. We are comfortable holding each to account against what we have agreed to deliver. 3. Team members understand goals and objectives clearly, and they are committed to delivering them.			
Strategic Plan	1. We have a strategic plan that shows how we will deliver our core purpose. 2. Our strategic plan explains the main pillars of operational activity that it contains, and every deliverable within it is described using the SMARTER approach (specific, measurable, achievable, realistic, timebound, ethical, recorded. 3. We stick to our strategy, even when it would be easier to divert our resources to new things, until we all agree to change our strategy to add in new things and take out old things.			

Figure 4: The STAR MODEL® questionnaire 2017 – 2019, People & OD Partners Ltd

work on. Furthermore, we now have a similarly robust Maturity Matrix (more of this in Chapter 11) that we have developed, which maps any team's current and desired levels across the range of indicators. This is calculated by the way they answer questions and the scores they give for a question, for one element or for the whole questionnaire. We have also narrowed the questions down to the most important 16; two questions for each of the final eight elements in the STELLAR MODEL®.

As for the paper-based questionnaire, a data collection method that we used for some time, we were able to analyse it live, working with the session attendees so that they could see their results. This helped us support them to agree the priority areas that they would like to work on as a team to improve their performance. This was the process we used to develop a series of workshops for them over six to twelve months, with a range of exercises and experiences that they could move through, learning about themselves and each other along the way.

Whilst this might seem rudimentary on some level, it also proved to be highly successful for a whole range of clients who had not had this level of introspection either at all or for some considerable period. We worked with some of the largest NHS organisations in the UK, ambulance services, Foundation Trusts, and some of the largest regional and metropolitan borough councils in the period, as well as public healthcare in Australia. Many of these clients will go down in our archives as some of the most successful, well-evidenced, and outcome-driven interventions we have delivered. In Part Four, we provide you with the questions we ask now to assess each element of the STELLAR MODEL® and our Maturity Matrix, on which we plot the outcomes. This enables us to have a robust baseline at the start of our work and somewhere to aim for in agreement with the client, as well as the ability to review either at the end of the work or again at six or twelve months after we have exited.

As the next couple of years rolled on to 2019, and as the results and outcomes from the STAR team continued to be positive, there were more calls for our written work (blogs, articles, and a book) to support this, and we sought to trademark the name.

The legal process is fairly time consuming, and as STAR is quite a well-used name, it was going to prove problematic to link this to our model and continue to use it, so we adopted a similar title, that of STELLAR MODEL®, and this passed through both the Australian and International Trade Mark process without issue. We then had the protected intellectual property of a leadership and team coaching model called the STELLAR MODEL®.

Between 2019 and 2022, the STELLAR MODEL® has seen several revisions, as outlined in Figure 5 (over page).

In 2019, as a result of our ongoing collaboration with Diane Wilkinson from Connecting to Excellence in the UK[14], in our desire to widen the use of the STELLAR MODEL®, we worked together to improve how the model might be interpreted by clients. With Diane's help, we were able to be clearer about what each of the seven elements were referring to, which models underpinned each element, and the exercises we would use with clients to support their development in each area. Diane has gone on to successfully use the STELLAR MODEL® with a range of her clients from the public, private, and third sectors, so we know it easily translates across sectors. For some time, the model in Figure 6 (page 19) was used extensively to support the development of high performing teams.

By 2021, we felt, as we tuned into client feedback and kept up to date with developments in our field, that there was something missing. One key

14 Connecting to Excellence (2022). Connecting to Excellence, Team Facilitation and Executive Coaching. Available at https://www.connectingtoexcellence.com/

STAR	STELLAR 2019	STELLAR 2021	STELLAR 2022
The WHY of the team			
Core Purpose	Core Purpose	Coure Purpose	Purposefully
The WHAT the team do			
Decision Making	Making Decisions	Making Decisions	Decisively
Accountability	Delivering Accountability	Delivering Accountability	Accountably
Strategic Plan	Planning Strategically	Planning Strategically	Strategically
The HOW we do it as a team			
Behaviour Code	Behaving Well	Behaving Well	Kindly
Conflict	Embracing Conflict	Embracing Conflict	Curiously
Trust	Developing Trust	Developing Trust	Vulnerably

Figure 5: The evolution of the STELLAR MODEL®

word that kept coming up when Diane and I were working with teams was clarity. Clarity of thought, decisions, communications, role, etc. We decided there needed to be something more in the model regarding the need for leaders and leadership teams to be clear. We decided to add an additional element: CLARITY. A short and simple word that expresses what we have found, time and again, that is often missing from leaders and leadership teams. Why do we humans so often feel the need to add lots of fillers around what we really want to say? We seem to think that this is kinder, that it softens the message, but it is confusing, unclear, and disrespectful. As Brené Brown

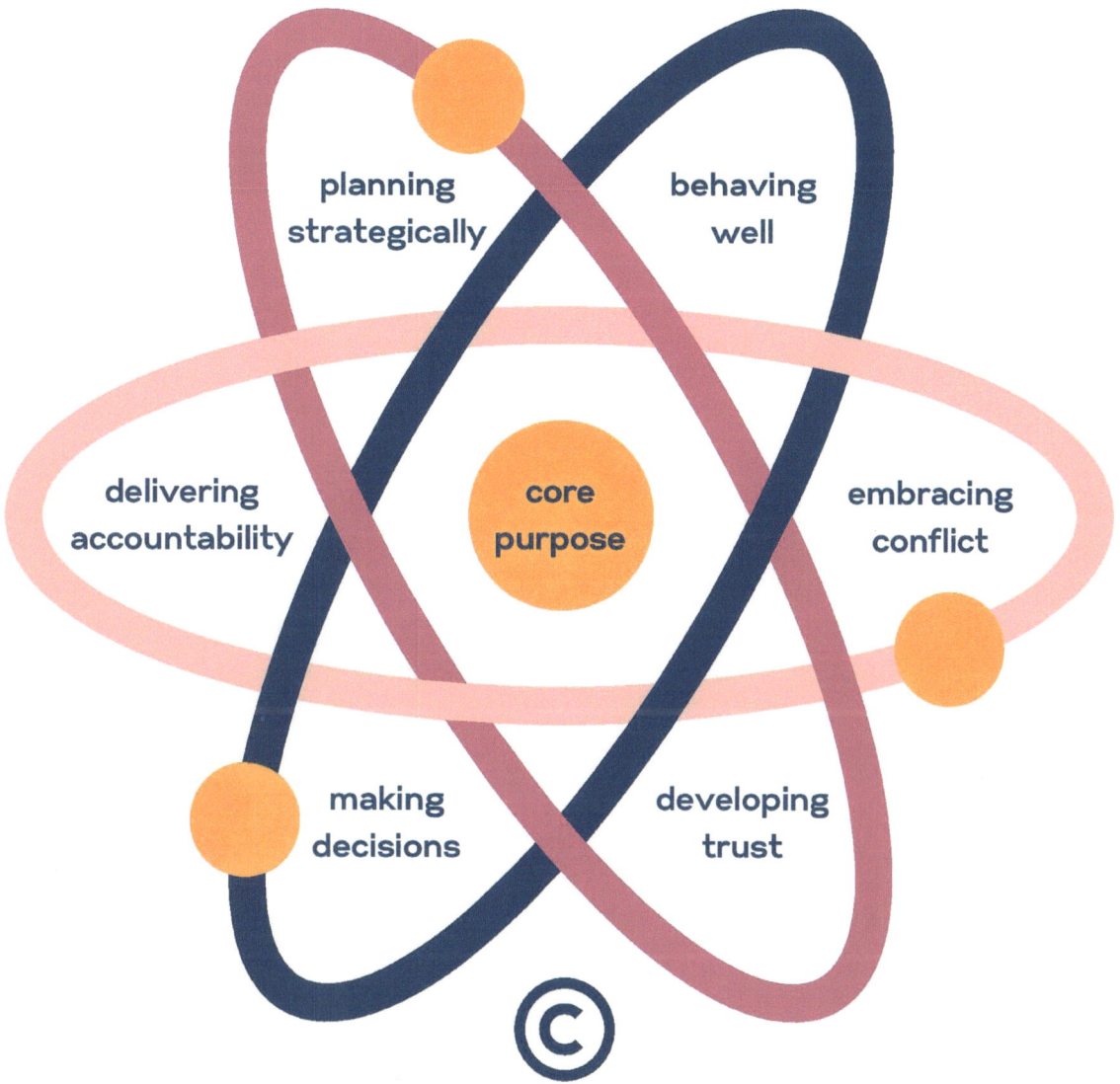

Figure 6: STELLAR MODEL® 2019

points out, "Clear is kind and unclear is unkind[15]. We add the fillers to make ourselves feel better. We might not recognise that, but it is true; we are more comfortable adding packaging to a hard truth than just offering the truth and the clarity with love, care, compassion, and understanding.

Our interpretation of clarity, if it was to be a new element of the STELLAR MODEL®, pulled together what we wanted to see in leaders when they were giving messages to each other and to their wider team members, and it covered clarity of role for the whole team and for each individual working within it.

To fit in with what we already had in the current STELLAR MODEL® (two

15 Brown, B. (2018). Dare to lead: Brave work. Tough conversations. Whole hearts. Vermilion.

words to describe each element), we went with "Providing Clarity". This gave us eight elements in total: the central element and seven surrounding it.

Interestingly, we had agreed with Munu that he would paint his version of the STELLAR MODEL® with a central element (Core Purpose) and with the remaining six around the outside, and as he had started the painting, and we didn't want to interfere with his creative process and get him to change mid flow, we therefore decided not to mention to Munu that we had a feeling we needed an extra element! But guess what? As often seems to happen, the universe tends to unfold exactly as it should, and when we went to view and collect the painting, Munu had created it with the central element surrounded by seven elements. How fortuitously weird and somehow spiritual! He had known we needed another element.

As this meant we needed to revamp our graphics to represent the way Munu had drawn the painting, we reviewed the words we were using to describe the elements and wanted to be sure they all worked together, and they landed well with our clients. We decided to make it even simpler and reduce the names of each element to one word. Therefore, we happily have now settled on the shorter, more active names for each of the elements of the model.

- Core Purpose becoming PURPOSEFULLY.
- Planning Strategically becoming STRATEGICALLY.
- Delivering Accountability becoming ACCOUNTABLY.
- Making Decisions becoming DECISIVELY.
- Providing Clarity becoming CLEARLY.
- Behaving Well becoming KINDLY.
- Embracing Conflict becoming CURIOUSLY.
- Developing Trust becoming VULNERABLY.

A note on why we have chosen some of the new words in the STELLAR MODEL® 2022. Most of them will be self-explanatory, but it is worth explaining Kindly, Curiously, and Vulnerably somewhat.

KINDLY originally came from the concept of Behaving Well, treating others in your team well, respectfully, compassionately, etc. When we were recently working with a client group and they were deciding on a set of behaviours they could simply describe to their team, they went with the following:

Figure 7: Client's behaviour list created in a workshop

As we worked and they talked about what they meant by being kind, this resonated so clearly and simply with us and with what we meant by our previously used Behaving Well that we were moved to replace behaving well with Kindly.

The element CURIOUSLY (or rather the name change, to Curiously) is another recent change as we moved to use single, active words. This element has always been slightly controversial when working with teams as its route is from the previous Embracing Conflict. Some teams struggled to get used to engaging with the element due to the word "conflict", which is of interest as a phenomenon and often left lots open to be explored. However, in a recent discussion with a long-time collaborator, she was explaining that she was having a difficult time with a co-facilitator she was working with as they were doing "tell" a lot (meaning they spoke for over twenty minutes non-stop) and seemed to be running on ego and not being in listening mode, in service of the client. Our role as an OD consultant, team coach, or however you want to refer to it, isn't to promote ourselves or love the sound of our own voices by being on broadcast, it is to support the client to get to their aims, or in other words, "be in service of the client". Her comment was that she was trying her best to remain "curious". It struck us right between the eyes that what we had always meant by the Embracing Conflict element wasn't about full-on warfare, which is what some teams jumped to due to the way we had named this element. It was more a call to notice what is hooking into us about other people's behaviour, notice what is pushing our buttons, and remain curious;

curious about our response, curious about the behaviour that is showing up and where that came from, and retain a belief that, if we understood what a) drove their behaviour and b) drove our response, we would be able to achieve a meeting of minds around the behaviour through a process of kind feedback. Therefore, we agreed to change the element to **Curiously** rather than use any wording linking the element to conflict.

Finally, the last change we made to the naming of the elements was that of Developing Trust, which, for the 2022 version of the STELLAR MODEL®, became **Vulnerably**. We are huge fans of Brené Brown, whose whole work is based on revealing vulnerability and showing that this is a strength. To really trust each other, any leadership team must seek to create a psychologically safe space for all members and get comfortable with showing vulnerability. So, as we needed one word, and "trustingly" didn't seem to be a real word, we went with **Vulnerably**. And the model is complete, for now! The picture created by Munu is shown in Figure 8 and, as an artwork in its own right, is titled The Seven Clans, and the graphic representation of this (created by the fabulous Michelle) is shown in Figure 9. Later in the book, as we get to Munu's story, we will explain the meaning of the symbols he has used to represent the elements of the STELLAR MODEL®.

Figure 8: The Seven Clans - Munu Wuthuga Dardakiin, 2021

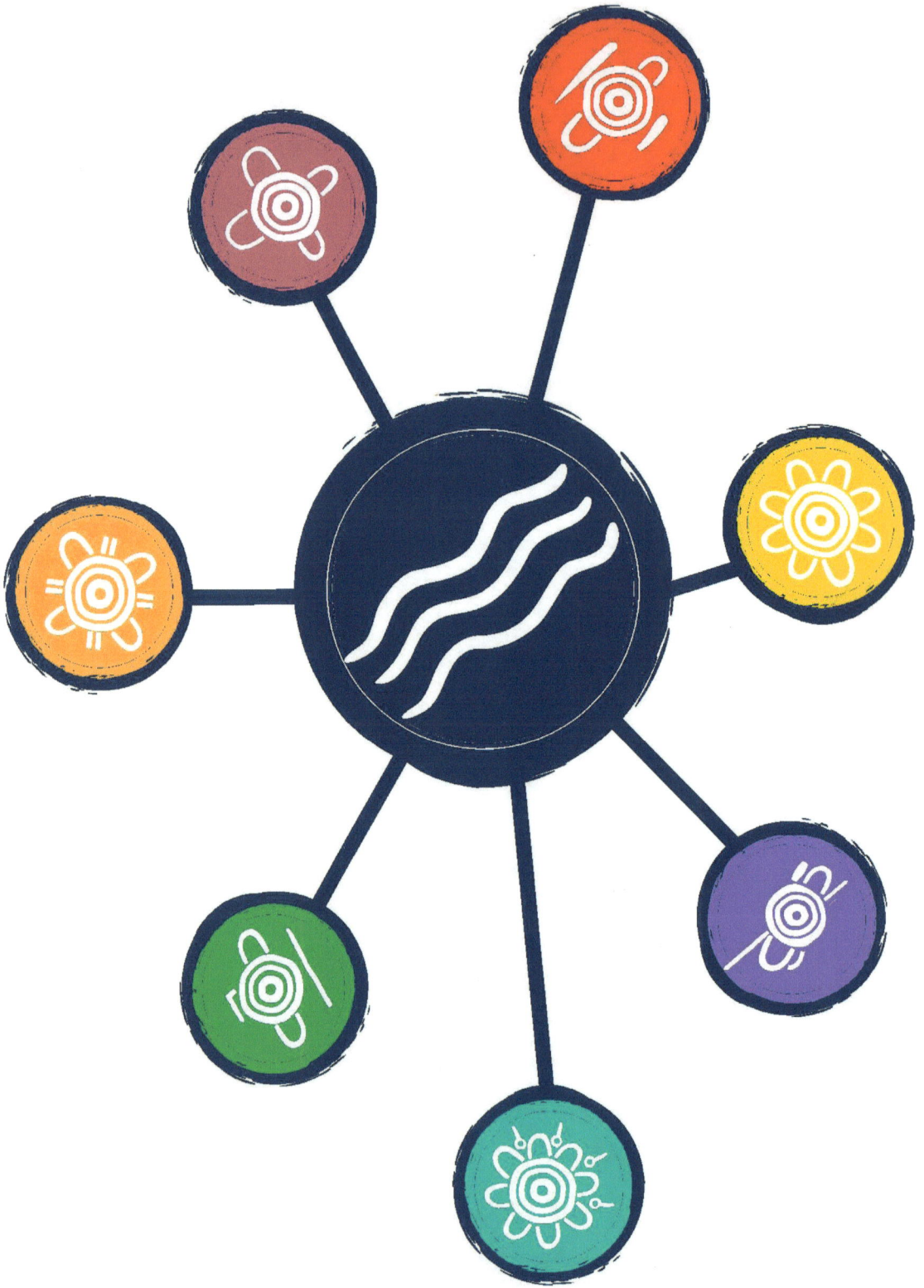

Figure 9: The STELLAR MOEL® 2022

CHAPTER 2

HOW WE USE THE STELLAR MODEL® WITH TEAMS

Time poor teams who come on an away day to work on getting tangible outcomes and who want to take part in a team development process need some practical advice and easily implementable tools to come away with; things they have created and can take ownership of, while at the same time working on their human relationships. That often means we must do some teaching about a range of concepts or theories before the team members can have an implementable take away. Therefore, once the gathering and analysis of data is complete, the team are able to prioritise the order in which they might need to pay attention to the different elements of the model and customise the teaching, the theories, and the exercises we work on with them to meet their needs and provide the outputs and outcomes they need for their development.

Only after some time did we realise the synchronicity of our approach with the Simon Sinek[16] approach: People will buy, or in our case focus on, your WHY before they focus on the how or what. The WHY of whatever you are doing is of vital importance. Much of our work is to bring leadership teams back to the WHY, or the purpose of their team. Many organisations or teams are quite clear about the WHY of their business-as-usual work, the WHY of their organisation, or the WHY of the team they lead (although, surprisingly, that is also often hard to agree on). But most leadership teams have often not spent any time discussing or agreeing on the WHY of their leadership team. What is the purpose of them being grouped together in the way that they are? Are they a team at all or are they a group? Should they strive to be a team and, even better, a high performing team? Therefore, it follows that if we are going to work with them on their development to being a high performing team, our first step is to support them to agree what their purpose is as a team. What is their WHY? This is the very reason that PURPOSEFULLY is the core of the STELLAR MODEL®; without a compelling WHY, a compelling purpose, it is quite hard to build a foundation for the rest of our work

16   Sinek, S. (2011). Start with why: How great leaders inspire everyone to take action. Penguin Books.

together. Once the understanding about working PURPOSEFULLY is developed and agreed, this supports further discussions on what the team need to do and how they need to do it.

So, at the very beginning of an engagement with a client, individual leader, or leadership team, or even when we work with a whole system, all the work we do is anchored around the team's PUPOSE, their WHY. This is so that all their work is done PURPOSEFULLY. For us, that means "done in service of their purpose". If the work they are doing isn't in service of their purpose, then what is the point of the work they are doing? Are they wasting time on nugatory work or is their purpose wrong? One of those two things must be true.

It is important to start there (with the agreement of their purpose) and get clarity, agreement, and a sense of simple understanding about the purpose of the team and anchor everything back to that guiding force, that compass, that north star. You can work all you like on the other elements, but if a team doesn't have a clear purpose and a strategic plan to deliver that purpose, then our work with them might as well be a hand-holding, campfire sing-along, which is lovely, but stuff won't get done.

For us, this presented the balance of providing a path or a clear direction with the heart that comes from being in a team that genuinely cares for each other. Below is a high-level overview of how we use this in our work with teams.

- Firstly - we focus on explaining the model to the team, gathering and analysing a wide range of data (individual, team, operational, organisational), and providing feedback on which part of the model they need to work on most.

- Secondly – we work with them on defining and understanding their purpose, to help them work PURPOSEFULLY, which is an anchor we come back to time and again.

- Thirdly – we work our way around the model, depending on what the data analysis tells us, but always covering all areas. We are supporting the development of the leaders and the leadership team across all areas with a range of practical and experiential interventions.

- Finally - we wrap up the interventions with a plan for sustainability for the team, and sometimes we will come in and do a health check with them at either three, six, or twelve months following our final workshop.

It is also worth stating here that the work we facilitate them to do supports the delivery of their outcomes, like a strategic plan, a risk appetite statement, or a values statement, i.e., real, tangible, required outputs using tools, exercises, and interventions that allow them to create outcomes by working through the eight elements of the STELLAR MODEL® and thereby improving their leadership skills individually and as a team, whilst getting what they might otherwise call "real work" done. Of course, we would say the effort put into their relationship as a team and their development as a leader is the real work.

The STELLAR MODEL® has been refined and developed with lots of teams internationally over the last ten years, and we are now ready to share it and teach others how to use the model, or elements of it, to develop their own teams.

CHAPTER 3

COLLABORATION IN ACTION

Figure 10: Dawn Jarvis. Author, Managing Director, People & OD Partners 2022

Dawn

Dawn Jarvis is an organisational development practitioner, specialising in supporting the development of high functioning senior leadership teams, mostly in the public sector and, on a smaller level, the private health sector. She has much experience as an executive leader, board member, and senior decision maker in the UK Senior Civil Service and the NHS. Dawn has been leading her own consultancy company, People & OD Partners, since 2014 (part-time at first, while still working full-time in-house) in the UK and across the UK and Australia since 2017.

Dawn is the youngest of five children to Pat and Eric, parents who were both public sector workers, and she was born and brought up in Liverpool in the UK, in a working-class household, where money was scarce and love was in abundance. Her values were set from an early age, and the tapes that still play in her head are along the lines of:

- **You can be anything you want to be if you work hard enough.**
- **Be nice to the people on the way up as you might meet them on the way down.**
- **Dress for the job you want, not the job you have.**
- **Do as you would be done by.**
- **Don't set out to hurt anyone and apologise if you do it by accident.**
- **What other people think about you is none of your business.**
- **If they are talking about you, then they are leaving some other poor bugger alone.**

In Dawn's early career, she had a brief fling with the armed forces, but, deciding it wasn't for her (she asks too many questions and has long since realised she is a terrible employee!), she went into retail management, working for a few big companies but couldn't quite get the commerce ideal. After being made redundant, she was like most people in the late 80s and early 90s who signed on and had anything about them; she was roped into working in a benefit office. What started as a casual contract in 1991 led to a life-long career, with a large part of it in the Senior Civil Service with the Department for Education (her eighth department with five house moves). During her time with the Department for Education, Dawn held posts such as Head of Equality and Diversity, Director of People and Change, Director of Corporate Transformation, and Program Director for Shared Services.

With a Human Resources background, Dawn qualified as a coach, coach supervisor, program director, and organisational development practitioner and went on to lead several machineries of government changes and several huge change projects across departments and supported the introduction of various new and contentious ways of working, gaining a Civil Service Award from Her Majesty the Queen in 2010 for a program she led, saving millions of pounds for the government.

In 2012, Dawn decided to change sectors to be at home more due to her growing family and took a post in the NHS as Executive Director of People and Organisational Development. This was a similar role, in a similar public sector organisation, and meant she could work twenty minutes from home rather than spending the weekdays in Westminster. But the culture shock was huge. Within a month of being in post, the Chief Executive (CE) that had recruited her relocated to Australia, and she worked with the Chair to recruit a new CE and virtually a whole new Board. This Board and Executive Team brought stability and structure to the organisation, and operational delivery, quality, and safety and Dawn's own people and OD team grew, developed, and won national awards. However, the financial situation across the NHS would prove to be too much, and the organisation went into a shocking financial meltdown. The default approach by the regulator at the time was to threaten the removal of the Executive Team and Directors and replace them with a turnaround team brought in at huge expense, paid for by the organisation, which was in financial difficulty. It made no sense to Dawn and her colleagues, so they decided to put another plan to the regulator. Rather than the tried and tested "bring in one of the Big Four Firms" approach, they put a plan together to do it them-selves, with Dawn taking the role of Turnaround Director.

Over Christmas 2015, Dawn Googled "financial turnaround", put an internal change team together and a two-year recovery plan in place, and brought in a few days of external support help from an experienced Turnaround Director. It was a long slog, and there is probably another book to be written about how to do a financial turnaround when you are not a finance specialist and when you work with the people in the organisation to make the decisions. However, to cut a long story short, within fifteen months, the organisation had met all the targets set for it by the regulator and Dawn was in demand to show other NHS organisations the process, which had, to a large extent (perennial and persistent historical NHS underfunding aside) worked.

Dawn left her full-time role in the NHS in March 2017 and pursued her solo career full time and has since worked for various primary care collaboratives, two UK ambulance services, many NHS Trusts and trust chains, other public and private healthcare organisations, and several local, regional, and metropolitan councils, predominantly in the UK and Australia. Additionally, People & OD Partners has bases and partners in both countries. While the main passion of the organisation is as depicted in this book (building high performing leadership teams in the public sector), Dawn also coaches one-to-one, supports Boards and Executive Teams with strategy development and governance, including risk appetites, and supports senior conflict resolution.

Dawn holds a master's degree in Human Resource Management, several Post Graduate Diplomas in Coaching, Coaching Supervision, and the Psychology of Coaching, and is working towards a doctorate on the use of questions in teams. She is a graduate of the Australian Institute of Company Directors, a Fellow of the Chartered Institute of Personnel and Development, and an alumnus of NTL. She is also wife to Tony (a teacher) and Mum to Jess (a mental health nurse) and Liam (a student with ambitions to be a police officer). She is a regular, if quite clumsy, runner, a lifetime Weight Watchers member, and a newbie self-taught crochetier.

Figure 11: Munu Wuthuga Dadarkiin

Munu

Hi to everyone reading this book. My name is Edward. My language name is Munu Wuthuga Dardakiin and my tribe is Dubbi Warra. We are from Hope Vale in Cape York, a part of the northern tip of Queensland in Australia. We are one of the last tribes that speaks its fluent original language. I grew up in Central Queensland for most of my life in a little indigenous community called Woorabinda.

I am now living on the Gold Coast in Southeast Queensland Australia and have been here for 11 years. I'm an artist and a healer, and I've been painting for a very long time now.

I've been working with plant medicine for a few years now, but I've always loved plant medicine, ever since I can remember.

I just started my business last year, doing the two things I love the most: healing ceremonies and painting. It has been fun so far, helping people from within and through painting.

Art has opened lots of different doors for me, which has been so exciting for me and my family. I've sold a few hundred paintings around the world that I'm very proud of. If you would have asked me twenty years ago whether this was what I would be doing now, I wouldn't have been able to say I knew how my life was going to turn out.

I am so thankful for my journey and achievements so far.

One of my best memories was of my childhood and Great Great Grandmother. Just being with her and around her. She was my teacher and is still such a big part of what I do now.

I used to love her stories about her people, her childhood, her country. She was from the Wide Eye people from near Cloncurry in Northwest Queensland. I'm so thankful and very lucky to have learnt from such a beautiful and amazing woman.

I love doing what I do with my culture and sharing knowledge with others. I hope this book and my collaboration with Dawn provides some strong roots for those leaders and leadership teams who head up organisations that provide services to my people and want to be better and do better as leaders for the communities they supply and the cultures they serve.

Figure 12: Dawn and Munu, April 2022, Gold Coast, Australia

Dawn & Munu

After trying to find a route into working with several Queensland and Gold Coast-based aboriginal councils or groups, Dawn was getting a bit despondent with herself, feeling that a collaboration with an indigenous artist and storyteller would never happen. She was concerned that she wasn't explaining what she wanted to do well enough as she just hadn't been able to make the right connections.

Dawn was also concerned that she didn't know enough about the indigenous culture of Australia to even be asking the right questions. But as has been usual throughout her life, the universe placed before her the right door to open at exactly the right time. Dawn has found, time and time again, that she seems to be placed in the right place at the right time to pick up an opportunity that is waiting for her.

One Sunday, as she was walking along the foreshore in Coolangatta[17], she saw a man displaying a range of amazing artwork on the grass at the top of the beach and she went and had a chat; a chat about his art, a chat about whether he would be up for a collaboration, and whether he was interested in a longer chat about being commissioned to create the artwork for a book. Munu was happy to have the chat, and Dawn took his number. About a week later, they met up for a coffee; well, Dawn had a coffee and Munu had a hot chocolate!

Dawn explained the model to Munu and talked about what she was trying to do, and it just seemed like Munu instantly understood. Munu took Dawn's pen and drew a sketch in her notebook after hearing all about the model and seeing the graphics she used in her work to explain the model to her clients, which is shown in Figure 13.

---

17 Coolangatta (2022). *Destination Gold Coast*. Available at
https://www.destinationgoldcoast.com/places-to-see/coolangatta

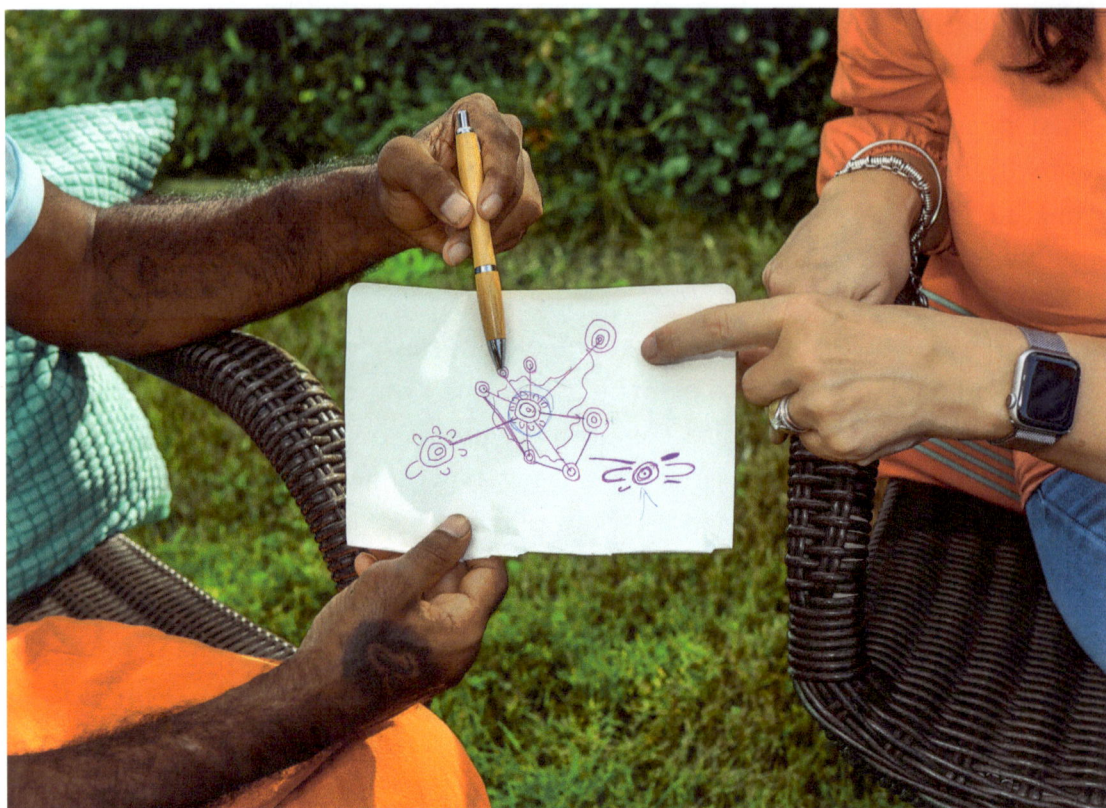

Figure 13 Original sketch of the idea for the painting.
Munu Wuthuga Dardakiin, September 2021

It was a meeting of minds and souls, and once again, Dawn's theory about the universe presenting what you need when you need it seemed to be proven. There followed some discussion about how the collaboration would work, a contract and agreement, and the commissioning of a painting, which all took a bit of time to work through.

Munu wanted to be in the project for the long term, which delighted Dawn, and so they agreed to pool their resources to kick it off the ground and split any profits made from the sale of the book fifty-fifty. They engaged a legal team to draw up the contract, so it was all official, and then Munu began the painting. Dawn went to view it and collect it in December 2021 and then began to do her bit, which was the writing.

PART TWO
NAVIGATIONS

Our Map
of the Content

CHAPTER 4

PURPOSE AND AUDIENCE FOR THIS BOOK

This book has been written for three audiences and therefore for three purposes.

Its first purpose is to record, catalogue, and put into order the work we have been doing with clients (as in-house and external practitioners) for over thirty years. There comes a stage in the careers of those who spend their time supporting, teaching, and coaching others when you know that you have amassed a collection of methods that work, that they deserve their own story, and that others might benefit from being told the story, being able to use methods, and seeing their magic at work. It follows that the first audience for this book is the people we have worked with over the years, who have asked us to write it down, and our families and friends, who often, let's face it, don't have the first idea what we really do. Hopefully, this will help explain!

Its second purpose is to prompt you, the reader, to continue to be curious about your own development as a leader, the development of your leadership team, or how you as an internal or external OD practitioner might support the development of leaders or leadership teams in your organisations in the future. It follows that the audience group here is leaders, leadership teams, and OD practitioners, whether internal or external.

Its third purpose is to show collaboration in action, i.e., the many collaborations that culminated in getting this book written. There is a whole section to say thank you to the people without whom this would not have been possible; if these people had not been open to the idea of fully collaborating, we would still be living with older and slightly less useful or clear versions of the STELLAR MODEL®. It so follows that the audience group here is people who want or need to collaborate, really collaborate.

Just a few words on what we mean by "collaboration".

Lots of teams, organisations, and systems have the aim of collaboration, but we are not sure that true collaboration happens all that much in practice. If we look first at the various ways that teams work, they can either engage in NETWORKING, they can engage in CO-ORDINATED activities, they can

CO-OPERATE, or they can COLLABORATE[18]; see Figure 14. The definition of collaboration in Figure 14 describes a state whereby new things are co-created. Organisations and teams often share information, exchange ideas, and get sucked in by the idea that they are collaborating, but one vital ingredient is usually missing from many attempts at what we might call "true collaboration". That is surrendering to the fact that, to collaborate, we must all give something up to get something new and better. There is no ego in collaboration!

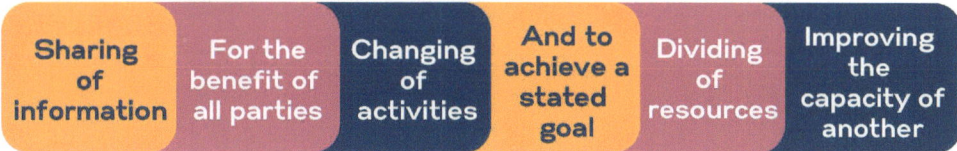

As well as ego, or what we might even describe as the fear of letting something go or the resistance to change, there are other systemic factors at play which hamper our ability, particularly in the public sector, to collaborate well, or at all.

We know first-hand how hard it was to disagree or challenge each other during the evolution of the STELLAR MODEL®, giving feedback on models and approaches we had all held dear for a long time to get a better outcome for us all to use.

NETWORKING

Sharing of information	For the benefit of all parties

COORDINATION

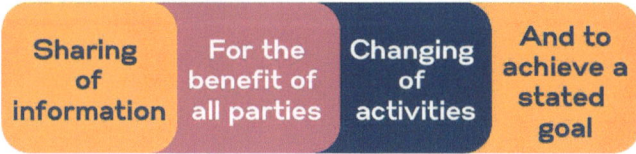

Sharing of information	For the benefit of all parties	Changing of activities	And to achieve a stated goal

COOPERATION

Sharing of information	For the benefit of all parties	Changing of activities	And to achieve a stated goal	Dividing of resources

COLLABORATION

Sharing of information	For the benefit of all parties	Changing of activities	And to achieve a stated goal	Dividing of resources	Improving the capacity of another

Figure 14: Huxham C, 1996, Creating Collaborative Advantage

18 Huxham, C. (1996). *Creating Collaborative Advantage*. London: SAGE Publications Ltd.

Factors causing what has been termed collaborative inertia[19] include lack of common aims, power struggles, trust issues, fluctuating membership structures, and leadership failures. Consider interdepartmental government committees where individuals are keen to contribute opinions and even potentially share information but then they don't follow through with promised action. Eventually, members cast off their role to more junior members with limited decision-making authority and it just becomes a tick box exercise where everyone colludes to say they are collaborating, but ever-changing leaders and chairs of committees result in a continuously changing direction and parliamentary election cycles result in a focus on short-term wins. Inertia is a disincentive that impedes outcomes and undermines motivation to invest in collaborative efforts in future.

In addition to collaborative inertia, organisational cultural norms and performance incentives often reinforce individualistic achievements over collaborative or group-driven outcomes. Hierarchical structures encourage positional power rather than joint power arrangements. This is further exacerbated by an implicit philosophy in Western societies that emphasises individual achievement. If this is not enough to undermine collaborative efforts, there is also overwhelming research evidence[20] that collaboration is a seriously resource-consuming activity. The overall benefits and outcomes need to be worth pursuing to attempt it.

Given the tangible barriers, the question remains: is collaboration even worth pursuing, and if it is, why? Of course we are going to say yes, absolutely, when it is appropriate.

For those of us involved in the process of creating the STELLAR MODEL® and this book, we know we have been collaborating in the true sense of the word, given that we can all attest to the fact that we have absolutely improved the capacity and capability of each other by challenging and supporting new thinking, by being able to give up some things we had worked on alone for some time, and by being open to allowing others to show their talents for the good of the project or the outcome.

19 Huxham, C. & Vangen, S. (2009) Doing things collaboratively: realising the advantage or succumbing to inertia? In: *Collaborative Governance - A New Era of Public Policy in Australia?* The Australian National University, Australia, pp. 29-44.

20 Huxham, C. & Vangen, S. (2009) Doing things collaboratively: realising the advantage or succumbing to inertia? In: *Collaborative Governance - A New Era of Public Policy in Australia?* The Australian National University, Australia, pp. 29-44.

CHAPTER 5

WAYS TO USE THIS BOOK

Your own purpose for deciding to read this book will determine how you choose to use it. You can use the contents page to look for the headings that interest you and head straight there, diving into each section as it suits, or you can read the book from cover to cover and absorb the whole picture, the whole story.

However you choose to use this book, it is worth knowing a little bit about the layout and having some navigational tips as these will provide you with a map to find your way around.

The book is split into five parts:

1. Introductions,

2. Navigations (where you are now),

3. Organisational Development – What is that all about, then?

4. The Seven Clans of Leadership (which contains our indigenous leadership story),

5. What next?

Four of these are straightforward. Read one line after another and proceed through the pages. The Seven Clans of Leadership is a bit different. After a short introduction, Part 4 starts at Chapter 10 with a story taken from indigenous Australian culture about a spirit called STELLAR, who appeared to the Elders of a tribe that was struggling to work together. The spirit called STELLAR explained what the Elders and the tribe of seven clans had to do to regroup and lay the foundations to thrive in the future. Chapter 11 relates this story to our current use of the STELLAR MODEL® as a tool for leadership excellence, either by individuals or leadership teams.

The remaining chapters in Part 4, Chapters 12 to 19, cover each of the eight elements of the model in turn, which all fit together to provide a synchronistic map for cultivating, developing, and maintaining high performing teams. Each of the chapters in Part 4 are laid out in the same way. Additionally, the edges of each chapter in Part 4 are colour-coded in the same colours we used in the model, so you can find your way to those pages quickly, using the model colours as your key – and it looks quite nice too!

In these chapters:

- Firstly - we **DEFINE** what we mean by the element, in this context, giving you a link back to the spirit of the STELLAR story.

- Secondly - we **EXPLAIN** what this element looks like in high performing teams and touch on some of the main theories we defer to when working with this element in organisations.

- Thirdly, we give you a glimpse of how we **INTERVENE**, highlight the exercises we use to support teams to develop their performance working with this element, and leave you with some questions and three top tips (for you, your team, and your organisation) that you might want to refer to when thinking about your leadership goals or those of your team.

If you are, therefore, really interested in all the practical applications of the model, then you can dive straight into the final part of each chapter. Here we give some practical exercise outlines, which show how we might work with leaders and their teams to develop their competence in each element of the model.

You might also be interested in our follow-up book (due out early 2023), which is a handbook for organisational development practitioners, providing the detail on all the tools and exercises we use when working with teams.

It would be nice to think that everyone picking up this book will read it all cover to cover, but if you read any part of it, and make a small change towards better leadership, we will be delighted!

CHAPTER 6

WHO MIGHT BE INTERESTED IN WHAT?

This book can probably be used by a whole range of people, and although it is aimed primarily at leaders, aspiring leaders, and senior leadership teams, it is hoped that organisational development practitioners and those supporting or facilitating leaders and leadership teams in organisations can also get a lot out of this book. The follow-up book will detail the planning and delivery of many of the exercises, templates, methods, and approaches that we regularly use and can attest to the impact of. This will be more specifically aimed at coaches, team coaches, group process facilitators, OD experts, and other such practitioners. The content included in this book should be enough to get you started and hopefully whet your appetite.

- **For individual leaders** and those who aspire to that responsibility, it is hoped that you will get tips, tools, questions to ask yourself, and, most importantly, time while you digest some or all of this book to think about how you show up as a leader.

- **For senior leadership teams**, it is hoped that you will work together to review where you are already strong, where you need to do some work, and how to come up with a plan to do that work. Being in a leadership team with the responsibility to lead others is a huge honour, and the collective role should not be taken lightly.

- **For those who support leaders and leadership teams**, it is hoped that you find some new ways to do what you have been doing undoubtedly well for some time. It may refresh some of your practice, introduce you to some new or different theories or exercises, and at the very least give you an excuse to try out some new tools with your clients. Go ahead, it will be fun!

To anyone who reads any part of this book for any reason, our call to you is that you notice what you notice when you read it. Consider your own reactions to the content we provide.

Do you agree with it or disagree with it? Does it make you curious, interested, excited to try something different or does it make you start to have some negative thoughts about your own performance so far? Does it validate for you what you are already doing as a leader or supporter of leaders?

We can't offer you any wisdom about whether any of your reactions are right; actually, there isn't really a right response to this content.

Our hope is that it will evoke some thinking and provoke some form of action, be that growth, development, learning, or just some long-term pondering and curiosity.

So ready yourself - here we go!

PART THREE
ORGANISATIONAL
DEVELOPMENT

What's That
About Then?

CHAPTER 7

WHAT DO WE MEAN BY THE TERM OD?

Organisational Development as a concept, or OD (not to be confused with organisational design, although this can be used within OD), has been around since the 1950s, but it still proves difficult to fully explain what it is. This is for two reasons: firstly, it is still a developing field, or what you might call a "moving target", and secondly, it requires an understanding of several sets of knowledge (behavioural sciences, change, social systems, the role of a third-party change agent), united by an underlying philosophical belief and value system. Hence, there are numerous definitions that can be applied. One we particularly like is:

> *'Organization Development is a system-wide application and transfer of behavioral science knowledge to the planned development, improvement, and reinforcement of the strategies, structures, and processes that lead to organization effectiveness.'*
> *Cummings and Worley, 2015[21].*

It is different from leadership development, human resources approaches, coaching, training, etc. (although they too can be part of the tools it uses), as it takes a whole system approach, and it is used to improve the whole organisation's effectiveness. However, it is important to understand that OD isn't just learning or development that is done to make people feel that they are being invested in. Although that is a great by-product, it also speaks to the sceptics of all that "pink and fluffy, kumbaya stuff" as it is directly linked to supporting the delivery of the bottom line or the required operational outcomes.

OD is magical. When it is done well, by skilled, powerful, compassionate practitioners, there is absolutely magic at work. The magic comes from the human spirit doing good things. When we bring together the whole system (clients, customers, consumers, critics, stakeholder, staff, managers, and so on), with as much diversity as possible (diversity of experience, knowledge, life,

---

21 Cummings, T. G., & Worley, C. G. (2015). *Organization development and change.* Stamford, USA: Cengage Learning.

exclusions, and setbacks), and bring out the common ground, we can build better futures. When people work on something together, they are vested in making it a success. That is why OD done well works for organisations where previous attempts at change management have failed or been done badly. Any organisational change project imposed from the top never works, at least in the long term.

We describe OD, or what we do in organisations, as "the use of behavioural science theories and tried and tested practical methods to deliver planned improvements in relationships, involvement (or engagement), ways of working, and outcomes". We have a process that we follow, which takes its lead from action research[22]. This is known as the OD Cycle[23]. We have shown our interpretation of the OD Cycle in Figure 15. Depending on what you read and defer to, the OD Cycle may have a different number of elements.

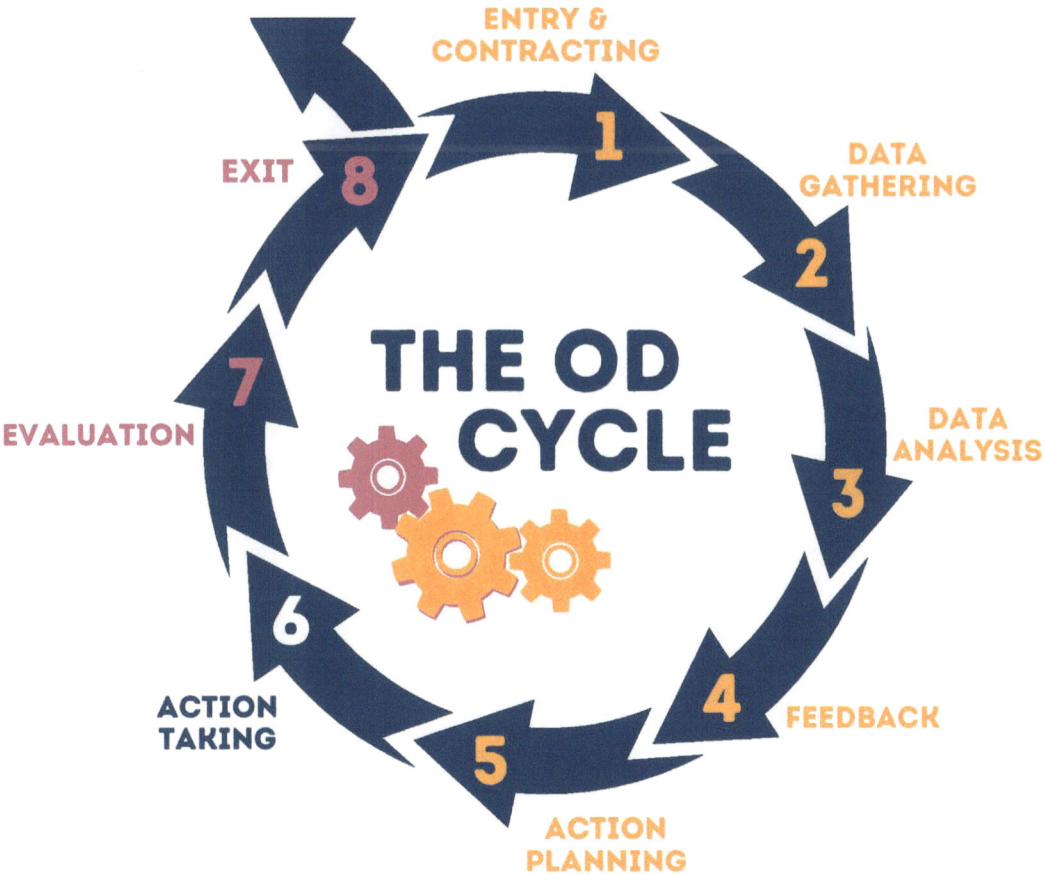

Figure 15: The OD Cycle

22 Lewin, K. (1946). Action research and minority problems. *Journal of Social Issues*. (2) pp.34-46.
23 Clark, P. (1972). *Action Research and Organizational Change*. Joanna Cotler Books.

Traditionally, there are six elements[24], but there are up to 10 elements in Cheung-Judge's work[25]. For us to practically explain to our clients what we are doing in our work with teams and why we are doing it, we settled on the eight elements in our process flow, as these seem to routinely make sense to our clients and pull from the fabulous work of Ted Tschudy[26].

Those of you who are time-served OD practitioners, you might want to skip this section, Part 3, or you might want to revisit your practice and check whether all the things in this cycle are still showing up in how you work.

The headlines of our eight phases of any OD engagement are provided below, but as this isn't a book on OD as such, references are given for excellent books, articles, and gurus that can provide lots more detail about OD as a practice and about the eight phases discussed here.

Phase 1 - Entry and contracting[27]

This begins with the initial meeting between the client and the practitioner, whether the practitioner is internal or external. An agreement is reached between the two of them about the presenting issue/s, the potential approaches, potential solutions, the time to be taken, the budget, financial arrangements, and other transactional or contractual agreements that will take place. Contracting and re-contracting should take place time and time again through the whole engagement to ensure expectations are still being met and boundaries are still being maintained. We can often be heard referring to "contracting with a small c" and "contracting with a capital C". For us, the capital C refers to the more transactional contract about the money, time, resources, etc. The small c, for us, refers to the contracting we do around the way we work, our expectations of each other and the work, and how we will measure success. Some clients find it easier to understand when we separate the two, but of course, for us, they both go hand in hand. But we could tell you a few stories about where we have got our contracting and boundary setting completely wrong over the years!

24 Davidson, D. (2005). The Organisational Development Cycle: Putting the Approaches into a Process. In E. Peck, *Organisational Development in Healthcare: Approaches, Innovations, Achievements.* (1st ed., p. 63). Taylor & Francis.

25 Cheung-Judge, M.Y. & Holbeche, L. (2015). *Organization Development. A Practitioner's Guide for OD and HR.* (2nd ed). Kogan Page: London.

26 Tschudy, T. (2014). An OD Map: The essence of organization development. In B.B. Jones and M. Brazzel, *The NTL Handbook of Organization Development and Change.* (2nd ed., p.129). San Francisco: Wiley.

27 Jones, B.B. & Brazzel, M. (2014). *The NTL Handbook of Organization Development and Change: Principles, Practices, and Perspectives.* San Francisco: Pfeiffer.

As the OD practitioner, it is our responsibility to be fully aware of bound-aries, power, control, and values. Ted Tschudy writes very well about these areas and other things to be mindful of in the text we cited earlier.

Phase 2 - Data gathering[28]

True to its action research roots, OD practice is data-based. Any practitioner worth their salt won't agree to "come in and do a one-off workshop" unless they have agreed that it is a facilitated learning session (not OD per se) or more of a lecture on principles or theories. They won't agree unless they are able to do some data collection to ensure they enter the system they are working in with the right level of knowledge to help the system get the best out of the session. Julie A.C. Noolan (2006) is one of the best writers on data gathering in OD we can think of, hence her being referenced here (she uses the term "diagnosing organisations", which we take to mean a combination of data gathering and data analysis).

Data gathering can take many forms. We can find out a lot about the individuals we are working with and the organisation by conducting interviews and group sessions or by carrying out questionnaires, psychometrics, other diagnostic tests and reviewing operational data and recorded decisions. Don't limit the sources to what is right in front of you; look as wide as possible across the organisation to give you the best view. This list isn't exhaustive, and which data sources are chosen depends heavily on the conversation and agreements reached in Phase 1 (entry and contracting).

When we are using the STELLAR MODEL® with teams, we will always get them to complete our questionnaire at the start and end of an engagement to show the movement they have made in their team maturity levels. Later, in Chapter 11, when we talk about our application of the STELLAR MODEL® in more detail, we will provide the questions we ask in relation to each element and how we map teams onto our Maturity Matrix. There are three really important things to bear in mind when data gathering:

- Diversity – don't limit yourself to one type of person, one site, one professional group; keep asking and thinking, "who else, who else, who else" should I be talking to? What else, what else, what else should I be asking?

- Lenses or frames of view – don't limit the discoveries you might make by only looking at the organisation through one lens or one frame of

28 Noolan, J.A. (2006). Organization Diagnosis Phase. In B.B. Jones and M. Brazzel, *The NTL Handbook of Organization Development and Change*. (2nd ed., p.192). San Francisco: Pfeiffer.

reference. Julie Noolan talks about four frames: structural, human, political, and symbolic. But are there more?

- Sixth sense or Gestalt interpretations – we should, as interpretive instruments of human behaviour, tune in to how it feels to be inside an organisation and what the whole picture is telling us. Notice what our physical, emotion, and mental reactions, our gut reactions or instincts, are telling us, as well as all of the factual data we will be gathering. Our perceptions will be vital, as long as we notice what we might be predisposed to notice (based on how we are hard-wired) and seek to notice things outside our usual frame of reference.

Phase 3 – Data analysis[29]

Analysing the data that is gathered in Phase 2 (data gathering) is an important part of the process. Whether this is number crunching the quantitative data that has come from surveys or interpreting the qualitative data from open-ended survey questions or interviews, the most important thing for the OD practitioner is not to make any assumptions and to remain curious. Our role is to make it very easy for the client to see and understand what we have found. Our approach has always been to treat all the data as the individual's and the organisation's property. This means that the words which members of the organisation use are used for a good reason and those words have their own story to tell (see more on dialogic OD[30]). Therefore, we hardly ever change any of the words, roll people's comments together, create themes from their open-ended comments. We see this rolling up, categorising, or theming a lot in others' work. There might be ten comments all worded differently, and the facilitator will review them and decide that they are similar, then suggest a theme that the group might want to work on, such as communication.

We remain curious about the purpose that this serves for the practitioner and the organisation, as lots of useful nuances and detail might be missed when themes are drawn by someone outside the organisational construct. We feel that it assumes a position in the system that we don't believe is helpful for keeping the boundaries of the ownership of the work and, in this case, the data that gives us our current state. It can therefore have the potential to inhibit

29 Hodges, J. (2020). *Organization Development: How Organizations Change and Develop Effectively.* London: Red Globe Press.

30 Bushe, G. & Marshak, R.J. (2014). Dialogic Organization Development. In B.B. Jones and M. Brazzel, The NTL *Handbook of Organization Development and Change.* (2nd ed., p.193). San Francisco: Wiley.

real movement in the system we are supporting. This is because when people see their words represented back to them, they feel a connection to having been heard, and that connection can be worked with to enable them to own the process of data gathering, the process of creating the change required, and the implementation of that change. If we take their words, theme them up ourselves, and so reinterpret their feelings, we might miss that mark, and we have almost certainly taken ownership of their process, their work, at this point.

For quantitative data, it is easy to analyse this and provide clear cut, definitive outcomes. It is factual that things are usually one way or the other. However, for open-ended comments and answers to questions in interviews, as previously mentioned, we have never thought it right to summarise or theme them up, precis, or alter what someone is saying.

It is of course the case that theming is needed to create consensus, alignment, and future focus, but, as you know by now, it is our view that this is the client's work, and our responsibility is to help them do that work, not do it for them. To summarise, reduce, or alter it would be taking ownership of the meaning, and as OD practitioners, we should always remember that it isn't our work; it is the clients work, their words, and their meaning. We are but creators of the safe space and curators of containers within which they do their work.

The only time we alter anything (with the contributor's agreement) is when a comment might be overly inflammatory, personal, or might identify the person saying it or who they are saying it about. Even then, we talk to the person about what they have said and agree with them regarding how it is going to be reported back and our purpose and intention of making the change at that early stage in the process. For example, during a data gathering interview, someone might say something like, "there is always an issue in meetings with Aneesha. She always makes negative comments about the work of my team in data analytics". Firstly, it would be important for us to agree how this was privately fed back to Aneesha. Secondly, we need to agree how this is surfaced in the team. In its raw state, it might not be helpful to the team to be used in the first round of group level feedback described in Phase 4 (feedback).

That doesn't mean it wouldn't be dealt with on many levels, it just means we would take care how it was handled in its raw form. We would build it into the group level feedback, but we might agree with the contributor that we would put a comment in the initial feedback along the lines of "there are often issues in our meetings when negative comments come from one of our teams about another team's work".

This allows the group to digest it; the sentence is still quite powerful, but it allows us to continue to build trust in the group and get to a place where the absolute specifics can be dealt with safely by the whole group. Gaining agreement with the contributor means they are likely to feel their input has been heard and is being dealt with and they understand the process we are going through more than if we had just gone ahead and depersonalised it without their involvement.

There are times to summarise the findings of the whole data analysis process, for example, if you are doing a presentation to senior leaders about a whole system, but not when dealing with teams consisting of individuals who have entrusted you to work with them in confidence.

Phase 4 - Feedback[31]

There are several elements to feedback, depending on what the data is telling us.

Firstly, it is important to loop back and recontract with the client leader. Often, there will be feedback specific to them, especially if they are the leader of the team, which must be kindly and clearly delivered. In your one-to-one interviews, you may have contracted that you will ask for feedback on the leader or it might just naturally come out, and once surfaced, you have a duty to use it wisely.

Secondly, it is polite and practically useful to give them (the team leader) an overview of the data before it is revealed to the group to:

a) Introduce them to the content,

b) Gauge their reaction so that they can be supported to work towards a reaction that will be in the best service of the group when the group get to see the feedback.

Again, we have all made choices in the past that we have learned from, and having a leader see for the first time several aligning views about them that could be seen as quite challenging can cause a reaction, which has the potential to cause some damage to the team and is hard, but not impossible, to recover from. It may cause a diversion or an additional session to work through the implications and some unnecessary suffering of individuals along the way, which could have been avoided if more care was taken at the feedback stage.

Thirdly, if there has been any psychometrics or other individual diagnostic tests and tools used, we would usually have carried out a one-to-one

31 Peck, E. (2005). *Organisational Development in Healthcare: Approaches, Innovations, Achievements.* Taylor & Francis.

debriefing session with each attendee to enable them to understand the report, the outcomes, and their own potential development needs before we get the group together. So, once we get the group in the room, we are feeding back the group's outcomes, looking through the lens of whichever psychometric we might have used.

Finally, the feedback session with the group needs careful planning. Often, this will be the first time the group and the OD practitioner have all been in the room together at the same time. Therefore, introductions, connections, and getting to know the exercises will be necessary to build trust in the process and the practitioner. Additional considerations will need to be made if this is a one-off session or the first session of several. These considerations will be along the lines of pace, depth, content, and the required outcomes that have been agreed at the entry and contracting phase (Phase 1). You may want to give an overview of the potential for the group if they choose to have future sessions by doing a light session covering all the elements of the STELLAR MODEL®, or you might prefer to dive deeply into one element to show the power of working at a deeper level.

This session can take several forms. Our usual approach, after contracting with the whole group about how we will work, explaining our "Ground Rules" for the session, and facilitating some group connection and trust building exercises, is to begin by providing the group with group-level feedback.

Assuming individual psychometrics have been completed, we would produce a team psychometric report and firstly relay that to the group, focusing on team and leadership styles of the group and the individual, looking at conflict styles and emotional intelligence and finally providing an insight into Myers Briggs®[32] or some other personality profile for the group and the individuals within it.

Then we would go on to do what we call a "Gallery Walk", an example outcome of which is shown in Figure 16. This is based on the assumption that we have run one-to-one interviews and/or focus group sessions for a large group bigger than around twelve to twenty people. If we have carried out the one-to-ones, we will have asked the individuals a range of questions, and we might have run several small focus groups with 10-15 people in each to get their responses to similar questions, for example:

- What is it like to be part of this team?
- What one thing would improve the way this team works?

32 https://en.wikipedia.org/wiki/Myers%E2%80%93Briggs_Type_Indicator

- What would you change if you were in charge?
- What is the best thing about working in this team?
- What frustrates you about how this team works? Why?
- What do you tell people outside the organisation about your workplace?
- What is your hope for the future of this team?

We would then produce a poster for each question, with the question placed in the middle and all the answers either handwritten around the outside or printed and stuck around the question. We really do prefer the handwritten approach as it feels more visceral and "real"; however, we are now getting very used to displaying this in all manner of online settings and getting people to interact with the answers on the day in person or online using Slido, Miro, MenteMeter, Teams, or any other version of the online OD space[33].

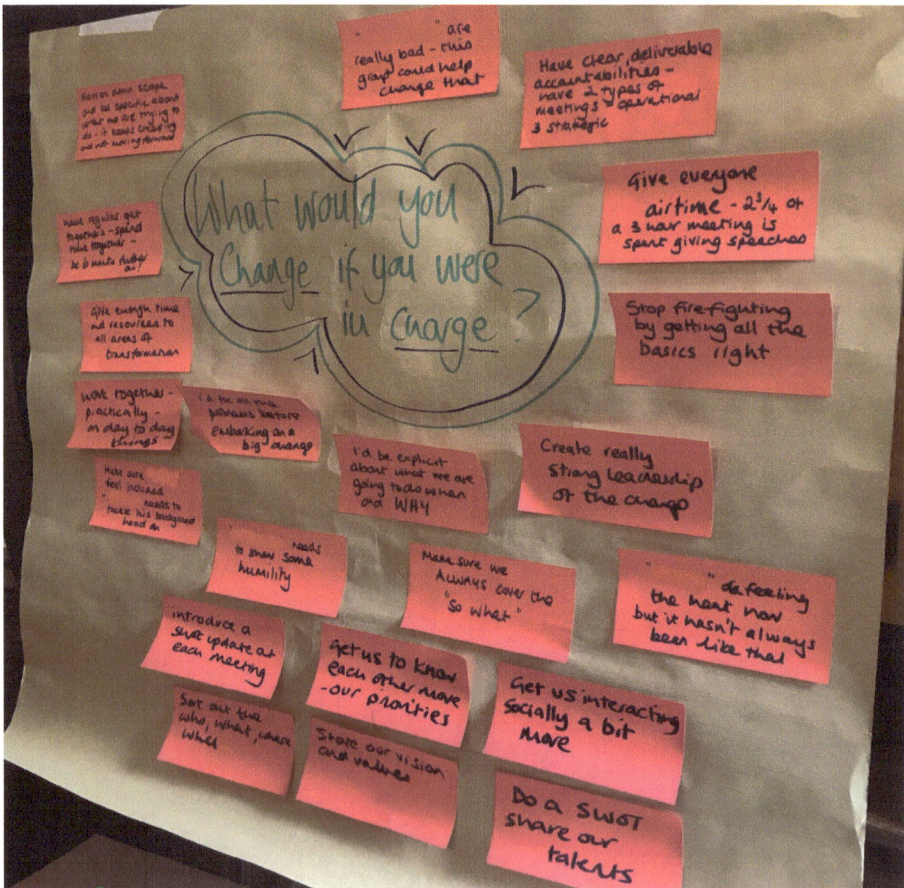

Figure 16: Client Example #1 Gallery Walk

33 Stirling-Wilkie, G. (2021). *From Physical to Virtual Space. How to Design and Host Transformative Spaces Online*. British Columbia, Canada: BMI Publishing

Phase 5 - Action planning[34]

Phases 5 and 6 (Action Taking) overlap very much, but it is important to remember the distinction between them and remember which phase you are in at any one time so that you can remain true to the OD cycle as much as possible.

Phase 5 action planning starts to take place as soon as you begin Phase 1, although be wary of going too far with any planning at that stage or you will have jumped straight into "solution mode", which may feel natural, especially if you are a self-confessed "fixer", but not helpful to the OD process or to the client system in which you are working.

The tendency to action plan before it is really the right time to do this will be present again as you are gathering data (Phase 2) or analysing the data (Phase 3) you have gathered. You can, to some extent, be forgiven for jumping to conclusions, making assumptions, and feeling quite pleased with yourself for knowing what is "wrong" with this system and coming up, albeit subconsciously, with a plan to fix it.

We have all done it; but again, it isn't helpful to your client and their system, as time and time again, we have seen that, when we do this, we are surprised by the direction the system takes when we begin to take action (Phase 6), otherwise known as intervening. Try your hardest to remain in true action planning mode throughout this phase.

Again, depending on the circumstances, there are a few ways to operate in this phase. You can discuss the potential actions with the client leader in the one-to-one feedback you will be doing in Phase 4 (Feedback), put a proposal together with some options, offer advice and a recommended course of action, and support them to make the right decision.

You can also suggest they form a planning group. This is particularly useful if you are working with a large system or large organisation. It relies on you getting a group together comprising of a slice of all locations, divisions, professions, and levels in the hierarchy to review the analysed data and consider the options going forward. This group would then also help plan any events, workshops, or other interventions and potentially be a reference group for the implementation of any agreed changes in Phase 6 (Action Taking).

Alternatively, and the method we use the most, we take the data, as described before in the Gallery Walk, into the room with the group or team. This is particularly useful for senior leadership teams of anything from around

34 Tschudy, T. (2014). An OD Map: The essence of organization development. In B.B. Jones and M. Brazzel, *The NTL Handbook of Organization Development and Change.* (2nd ed., p.129). San Francisco: Wiley.

five to twenty people. We show them the data and get them to analyse it and make some decisions about what is important to deal with and in what order. However, we have carried out this type of Gallery Walk exercise in a room of more than one thousand people and over several days in different rooms with ever-changing shifts of emergency department health care workers. This approach can work with very large numbers and with a rolling invitation list, it just needs careful planning. We might run a range of exercises to support the attendees to prioritise their comments. This helps to order the work going forward and help them to reach agreements on the outcomes they need to develop for the future.

They might prioritise by voting with coloured dots, as in Figure 17, or they might get into groups and take a poster each and "pitch" to their colleagues what they thought the group meant by their feedback and what they thought the action/s might need to be.

One consistent point here is that it is their work; they make the decisions. We don't theme, precis, or alter anything. They make the decisions on the work they need to do next, with support and challenge in equal measure from us. Our role might be to challenge if they are skating over issues or not being ambitious enough, just as our role might be to support if they need to have difficult conversations with each other to reach a conclusion.

Figure 17: Voting to prioritise during a Gallery Walk

Phase 6 - Action taking[35]

This phase is what some people think to be the only thing that OD practitioners do: facilitate and run workshops or stand up at the front and MC events. If you subscribe as we do to the view that "there is no such thing as a neutral question", then you have begun to "intervene" from the moment you have asked your first question of the system leader or the attendees in a one-to-one interview. Any survey creator will tell you that you can skew the answers you get by how you ask the questions. So, any time you dip your toe beneath the surface of the system you are intervening in by engaging with its members, you are "action taking".

However, given that this is the "front of house" part of being an OD practitioner, at least our clients could be forgiven for seeing this action taking phase as the intervention. Again, we use small i and capital I to differentiate in our world; capital I referring to the whole cycle and small i referring to a workshop or other carefully staged event. This isn't too important more generally, but when you are working at a macro and micro level, it is useful to remember which intervention type (the whole cycle, or the specific event) you are working on.

This misconception that the events are our main deliverables belies all the work and effort (which the client sometimes needs help in understanding is necessary) that goes into Phases 1-5. However, it could be said that this is the glamour end of the work, but boy can it be hard work to get to this phase, and it is definitely very hard work to hold a room of people for several hours in the safe space needed to effect change, let alone a full day or a week.

In our follow up book, we go into much more detail about how to plan an intervention, from concept to design, logistics, and exercises for each element of the STELLAR MODEL®, but here are just a few words about the Action Taking phase.

Timings, logistics, technology, stationery, location, and all things that can be planned well beforehand should be planned, reviewed, rehearsed, and planned again. Why? Because at the actual intervention, you as the group facilitator should be so present for the group and in service of the group that you will not want to worry about all the things that could have and should have been sorted. There will also be a huge array of surprises and unexpected happenings that occur with the attendees, and no matter how hard you plan, you will have to respond to these on the hoof, and having a counterpart, a support co-ordinator or co-presenter, will be invaluable.

35 Brown, D., Leach, M. & Covey, J. (2005). Organization Development for Social Change. In T.G. Cummings, *Handbook of Orgnization Development*. Thousand Oaks: SAGE.

Whatever kind of intervention you are running, be that a small group, team, large group, whole organisation, or system, we broadly follow the same design principles. These were given a process by Dick and Emily Axelrod from the Axelrod Group, and their book, Let's Stop Meeting Like This[36] is really worth a read. They use the term "the meeting canoe". Being based in Australia, we modified that to the Workshop Surfboard. Essentially, think of any object shaped with a larger middle and two smaller, pointier ends. See our version in Figure 18.

What we mean by using this shape is that, while we need to be mindful of welcoming people (welcome) in the room and online, this shouldn't take up too much time with long speeches, etc. Our next real task is to create a real connection (connect) to the task and between all the people present. Then we get them to reach an agreement on the here and now (discover), seek out the potential possibilities for the future and agree on them (elicit), decide on who is doing what going forward (decide), and make a good ending to the event with some reflection (attend).

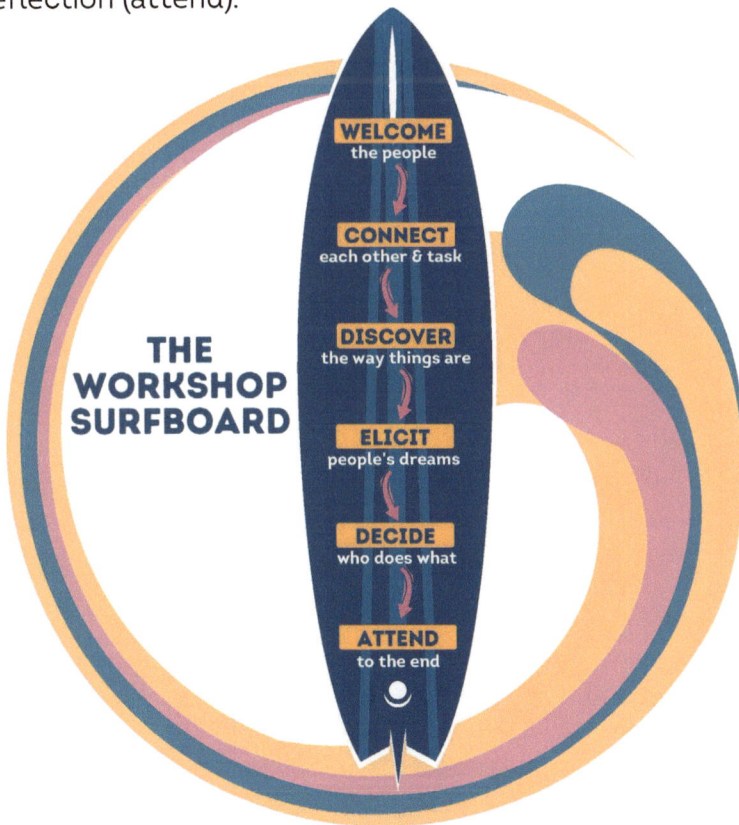

THE WORKSHOP SURFBOARD

WELCOME
the people

CONNECT
each other & task

DISCOVER
the way things are

ELICIT
people's dreams

DECIDE
who does what

ATTEND
to the end

Figure 18: The Workshop Surfboard – adapted from Axelrod's 'The Meeting Canoe'

36 Axelrod, D. & Axelrod, E. (2014). *Let's Stop Meeting Like This: Tools to Save Time and Get More Done.* San Francisco: Berrett-Koehler.

Finally in the section on this phase, we can't overemphasis enough that this is only part of the OD cycle, only part of the work; never allow your ego to take over and convince you that delivering sessions and holding a room's attention is the work. It is part of the work, an important part, but only a part of the work. And it isn't your work. You are holding the system you are working with in a safe container for them to do the work. When it becomes about you, you need to think about hanging up your OD spurs!

Phase 7 - Evaluation[37]

For many external practitioners, the delivery of a workshop or a session of any kind ends with an evaluation sheet (or an emoji in Zoom) completed on the day about the presenter, the food, or the room. A slight build on this is a follow-up questionnaire after the event, perhaps a month or so after, to see if any positive changes agreed to at the event have taken place. These can be great practices if you get the questions right, but we can enhance this.

This limited evaluation only speaks to the event itself, and there are many OD cycle interventions that might not have an event or might have multiple small group sessions, especially if we are seeking to support a whole system to collaborate. One workshop isn't magically going to make that happen. It is vital to remember the evaluation we are talking about here; it isn't an evaluation of an "event", it is the evaluation of the whole process, from entry and contracting through to outcomes. Entry and contracting is an intervention in its own right and should be planned and given enough time and respect, as should evaluation and exit. A successful evaluation is of great benefit to a client system, if done effectively.

So, what are we evaluating? All of the items covered in the early part of this section are really about evaluating actions or activities. How was the workshop? Did it meet your expectations? Was the food good? Was the room warm enough? All are valid questions to help plan future workshops in the same place or a different place. However, what we really want to know was: did the whole Intervention, with a capital I, from beginning to end, produce the results that we:

a) Thought it would?

b) Thought were needed to make the changes required in the system?

Some processes and outcomes should be evaluated, or maybe we could

---

37 Kirkpatrick, J.D. & Kirkpatrick, W.K. (2016). *Kirkpatrick's Four Levels of Training Evaluation*. ATD Press.

call them "input and output evaluation measures". For example, we would want to plan at the start, during contracting, what part of our evaluation is to be qualitative and quantitative, what data we might collect at the start and at the end, which valid collections tools and techniques might be used, and how we would measure outcomes and effectiveness of outcomes. Specific things we might measure could be:

- Resources – used to support the process, used to deliver the change, used in the future if nothing changes,
- Participation – in all the different process we might use, views about that participation, involvement in planning, and delivering any changes,
- Access and support – to and from leaders or system constraints
- Communication – up, down, out, and around before, during, and after our Intervention/s.

Examples of some hard outcome measures could be:

- Did production or output/outcomes increase?
- Was there a measurable and long-lasting change in work procedures?
- Is there now a different and better, more efficient and effective structure?
- Is there increased awareness and engagement?
- Has there been a creation of policies, processes, etc., that will ensure progress?
- Is there a new climate of openness and sharing, collaboration and trust?

We are seeking to review the contracting: did we end up with what everyone thought was agreed? Did we re-contract at every stage? While we have added the references to Kirkpatrick's model for evaluation in this section, it is probably too narrow for the whole organisational development cycle given and is more specifically focused on evaluating training and learning interventions and not organisational change or culture shifts. However, it gives us a good basis to start. What Kirkpatrick is looking to find out is:

1 - Results: did the training influence performance?

2 - Impact: did the training change behaviour?

3 - Learning: did learning transfer occur?

4 - Reaction: did the learners enjoy the training?

If we swap out "training" in one and two above, for the "organisational development process", this can be a useful framework for evaluation, apart from two points. Firstly, we must remember that we are evaluating all parts of the OD cycle (not just one workshop or event), and secondly, the word "enjoy" isn't used on its own. While we might want people taking part to enjoy some or all of the OD intervention, they should also feel challenged, stimulated, and occasionally downright uncomfortable if the intervention is going to be successful.

Phase 8 - Exit[38]

While it is sometimes tempting to continue with an OD process indefinitely in an organisation or a system and for as long as an organisation is willing to pay for it, there is always a good time to part company. Staying around too long as an OD practitioner can make you part of the fabric of the organisation, and how can you then not be part of the problem? Collusion builds up, blind spots appear, and you don't then have the distance to be objective and of best use to the client system. However, if you are an internal OD practitioner, you live this all the time and you can still do some great work for the organisation. In general, though, you will have contracted at the start of the process for a set piece of work, a set outcome, or a set period of time, and one reason for planning an exit is that this end is coming onto the horizon. Our job then is to create a handover plan, a set of documents, and to have transferred some skills into the system that leave the client set up to sustain the work in the future.

Another reason to plan an exit is if the work isn't working. For example, if the practitioner is putting more effort and energy into the work than the client, if agreements are made and then broken about what work will be done, or if the client system has already made the leap forward and no longer needs the work.

The general approach or philosophy of an OD practitioner should always be to leave the client system in a better place than it was before we entered it. The "first do no harm" part of the Hippocratic Oath[39] comes to mind here,

38 Weisbord, M. (1985). The organization development contract revisited. *Consultation: An An international journal*, 62 (2), 142-148.

39 Green B. (2017). Use of the Hippocratic or other professional oaths in UK medical schools in 2017: practice, perception of benefit and principlism. *BMC research notes*, 10(1), 777. https://doi.org/10.1186 s13104-017-3114-7

or even better, the Star Trek Prime Directive[40], which "prohibits any Starfleet officer interfering in the normal development of any society". This sounds like it might be at odds with what an OD practitioner is there to do, however, we mean several things when we say this, such as:

- Be exceptionally open with how we are working – so that the client can keep using the tools when we exit.

- Be exceptionally generous with our models and our collateral – so that they don't have to recreate handouts, worksheets, or how-to guides

- Be a teacher, a coach, and a supporter of internal staff who can carry on the work when we leave – so that there is real skills transfer across the system in which we are working.

- Never try to take the system to a place it isn't ready to go – our job is to create psychological safety and therefore a safe container in which to hold the team while we are working so that we can support the team to peel the next layer away and go deeper when there is a need.

- Meet the system where they are – so if they are hyper-stressed or reeling from an externally imposed change or directive, work with that first before attempting to do deeper work with the team. The prevailing noise and chaos first need to be absorbed or dissipated, at least enough to allow focus on any longer-term work or perennial issues that need to be addressed.

The planning of our exit is important; just as important as all the other phases of the OD cycle. Just as we wouldn't rock up to do a workshop without having done any data gathering or analysis, so too we wouldn't just end the workshop and say, "See ya, nice working with ya, be in touch if you need anything else".

We would have agreed at the start that our exit might be something as simple as a post-event report, handing over all the documents and collateral, or it might be more comprehensive, such as running surveys again, carrying out "train the trainer" sessions, or analysing outcome reports.

This is a time to keep our antennae on alert and notice our own and our clients' responses to this ending phase. It might be obvious to all parties that there is more work to do in the client system. It is often the case in the work we do that, at this stage, we are asked to do more work. What often happens

40 Wikipedia. (2022). Prime Directive. Available at: https://en.wikipedia.org/wiki/Prime_Directive

when people see the power of what true OD done well can do is they want more across a wider part of their system. It may also be true that the first OD cycle of work in this part of the system, that this group of people have experienced, has created a much stronger, more trusting team, which means that they can go around the OD cycle again in an even deeper way, uncovering more things that need attention. It may have been the case that you, as the practitioner, couldn't safely work on some issues as the team was too immature in its formation or in the individuals' development, or they weren't yet prepared to be as vulnerable as they might have needed to be to make the changes required. Don't be complacent about the knowledge or relationships you have built up with the client. You may think that you can shortcut a few phases or go directly into intervention delivery or planning, but this won't be in service of the client.

Make sure you at least wander through all the phases. It might be true that you don't need to spend as long in each, but to be clear, as you come out of the exit phase, you are moving straight back around to Phase 1, contracting and entry, or, to be more accurate, re-contracting and re-entry. This will require a new scope to be created, or it might be that a different part of the organisation needs work to be done in their part of the system or the same part of the system but at a different level of depth.

At this point, either the work will be done, for now, or you might decide you are not the right person to continue to work with the organisation going forward, in which case, an agreeable exit is brought about.

For us, this requires a handover report with a whole load of links and annexes for the work we have done, the data we have pulled and analysed, the slides and exercises we have used, and anything else that would be helpful going forward for the client to keep as a record of our work and for them to continue to use.

We are pretty clear that we want to add to the capability of the client system throughout our work that is agreed during the contracting phase. Therefore, Phase 8 will also be about evaluating whether our plans for doing this have worked as well as we expected (which might include sharing our tools and techniques, being shadowed by an organisational internal practitioner, training people on models and methods, or just introducing new ways of working and ensuring these are being practiced in the right way).

In addition, we will usually run some or all of the diagnostic tests and tools that we ran at the start to get a new baseline and invariably be able to show an improved position.

Our top tips for making this an extremely useful phase of work for our client and ourselves are as follows:

- Determine at the start of the cycle how and when it might end and what the end (or success, in some circumstances) should look like. This is just good contracting.

- Agree the practical aspects about what the end will look like; how do they want to receive the report? A presentation, etc.? Who will attend any meeting and what role they will play?

- Give overall feedback to the client and specifically the client leader with whom you contracted. This would be about your perceptions of how they handled the whole OD process. Stick to behaviours and be prepared with specifics and suggestions for improvement.

- Get feedback from the client, ask for specific examples, ask for behavioural examples, and seek input on how you might improve.

- Contract with the client about the future relationship you will have, such as coaching, mentoring, as an OD practitioner, or supplier of a service, and whether and in what format any regular check-ins might take place.

Concluding our whistle-stop tour of our eight phases of the OD cycle, our summary would be that all eight are important and should not be over-looked. Those that are often overlooked are vital to a good outcome for the client and integral to being an excellent OD practitioner.

CHAPTER 8

"BEING OD"

Being an OD practitioner is a strange occupation in many ways. We have to:

- Be fascinated by people's behaviour and not judgmental of it,
- Know what a client might need and not direct them to the answer but support them to find it themselves,
- Be confident to hold a client group at the edge of their comfort zone and have no ego about their destination.

It is a rewarding and joyous occupation filled with huge payback when you are able to witness those you work with being more, doing more, and blossoming in their roles. All this is based on being able to share with them some guide rails of theory, provide challenges to their current thinking, and support them when they stumble, while giving enough freedom for the discoveries to be theirs. What deep joy this brings!

"*We don't* do OD, *we* are *OD*".

Being an OD practitioner is, some would say, a calling, a vocation, a way of life.

Now this might sound a bit grand, but to do this work well, you need to be fully invested, have a predisposition to working in a certain way, and live your life by a core set of philosophies. There are two things that differentiate supremely effective OD practitioners from other organisational or facilitation interveners. We cover them both in some detail below. But let's first look at what the theorists say about the difference between a traditional facilitator and an organisational development practitioner, or a group process facilitator. We should also say that an OD practitioner could choose to do a stint as a traditional facilitator, had they not contracted with the group to allow them to intervene in the group process and therefore pay attention to the maintenance of the group's interpersonal relationships. We touched briefly on this in Chapter 1.

As an OD practitioner, we would be very interested in, curious about, and on high alert to notice everything we could about the group. The "notice what you notice" phrase is one we rely on a lot. What we mean by that is that it is important to be curious about what you are drawn to seeing. Is this because of your own issues, your own "hot buttons", experiences, transference, etc? Are you blinkered to some of the things you should be noticing because of your prejudices or because of other blockers?

Working with groups and teams, we view our job as "to notice" and we name what we notice so that we can reflect on that and work on ourselves and our own predispositions. We must be as open as possible to what we do notice, so that we are always acting in service of the client and not protecting ourselves or deflecting from ourselves.

If noticing is a skill all by itself, then adeptly naming is on a whole other level. Why do we say that? Well, it is one thing to observe a group and assess what we think from that observation all inside our own heads, but it is quite another to speak out loud, take a risk, follow our gut, and gracefully land something in the middle of the group that will both challenge and support them to grow and develop. It takes practice, confidence, and skill. The good news is, because it is a skill, it can be learned!

All groups have things to notice about them: those decisions that are not really made but put off while more data or information is sought; that one person who always makes a joke when a certain difficult topic is raised; that person who always interrupts, and so on. They will either push those issues under the rug as they are too hard to tackle or will have stopped noticing them because these issues have become their behavioural norm. Those norms will however be having an impact on the group's performance and the individual's (within the group) performance and/or levels of trust.

The OD practitioner will have talked to everyone in the room individually before the first group session and gained some insight into how the individuals feel that the group works. Some of the questions that help bring this out we have already shared, and they are things like, "what is it like to be part of this team?", "how do decisions get made around here?", "are there any bear traps I might fall into when I get you in a room all together for the first time?", and "how productive are your meetings?"

We might use a range of other methods to measure the group's effectiveness at the start of the engagement, from psychometrics to questionnaires (of which there are hundreds). We mostly use our STELLAR MODEL® questionnaire. We might also ask to observe a few business-as-usual meetings to get a sense of how the team work together. After a few minutes, they usually forget we are there!

Overall, when seeking to assess the effectiveness of a group, what we are looking for is:

- The degree to which the group's productive output (that is, its product, service, or decision) meets the standard of quantity, quality, and timeliness of the people who receive, review, and/or use that output,

- The degree to which the process of carrying out the work enhances the capability of members to work together interdependently in the future,

- The degree to which the group experiences contribute to the growth and personal wellbeing of team members[41].

Put in another way, when we are assessing or baselining the current effectiveness of a team, we want to know: does the team do the transactional job it was set up to do well enough and do the people in the team work well enough together for it to be worth their personal effort to stick together and worth the organisational effort to provide the support and resources to enable them to be group or team?

During the one-to-one sessions with the members of the team, we will explain our process and how we would like to use the information they are providing us. We find that the phrase "anonymous but not confidential" helps people understand that we will relay their information, but not whose information it is. It is important at this stage to see all the information but to see it attributed to members of the group as a whole, rather than individuals. We will talk about what a group process facilitator does and will seek permission from them individually, and then later, when we first get them together, we will remind them of the permissions they gave in their one-to-ones about how we might use the information they shared prior to the session and how we might intervene during the session. This means that we will use it in the first session as some feedback to the whole group about what many of them think in answer to the questions we have asked.

During the "in room" or "on screen" sessions with the team, we will focus on the **task processes** or "what" the team are in the room to do, as you might expect from any good facilitator. We agree the agenda, the timeframes, the tools, techniques, and exercises we will use, the ways we will engage the team, the ways decisions might get made, and what will happen with the information gathered, i.e., all the Post It notes on the flip chart or the comments in the

---

41 Hackman, R.J. (1990). *Work Teams in Organisations: An Orienting Framework, Groups that work (and those that don't).* Jossey-Bass

chat box at the end of the day.

As the team goes about working on some concrete outputs in various exercises, we support them with a workshop, and we notice their interactions. We must then skilfully decide what, of the things we have noticed, are important to raise with the team. We might notice some tension or some people holding back from conversations, and our entry into their conversation might be something like: "It seems there are some things that aren't being said. What might they be?" or "You don't appear to be answering each other's questions. You seem to be quick to change the subject when someone looks uncomfortable. Is that usually how your meetings work?"

This is our way of supporting the **maintenance processes** within the group. They are called maintenance processes because, just as a car needs maintenance, such as oil, water, and fuel, to run, so must a group. It must seek to meet individual members' needs if it is to work well without falling apart or ceasing to run. Therefore, maintenance for a team refers to the way in which types and levels of interaction, support, challenge, care, and behaviours show in the group in order to **maintain** the healthy nature of the group.

Maintenance can be split into three main areas, which we cover in a bit more detail below. It is always important to bear in mind that the issues each group faces shows its ability to reconcile the differing needs of members for participation, control, and warmth[42] so that their energies may be released for productive work. If the emotional needs of the members are not met, the energy of the group will be siphoned off and used to try to resolve the emotional issues in open or hidden ways, so us practitioners need to be skilled in dealing with covert issues and processes[43].

The key skills an OD practitioner needs to support maintenance processes should include the ability to observe and intervene in:

a) Participation and membership of the group: when, how often, and with what level of intensity we feel we need to belong to the group or be accepted by the group; how engaged or disengaged we are at any one time or with any one topic and the impact that our engagement or involvement in a discussion has on the other members of the group and therefore the outcomes of the group.

42 FIRO. (2022). *FIRO History and Background.*
   Available at: https://eu.themyersbriggs.com/en/tools/FIRO/FIRO-history
43 Marshak, R.J. (2006). *Covert Processes at Work: Managing the Five Hidden Dimensions of Organizational Change: Managing the Hidden Dimensions of Organizational Change.* Berrett-Koehler Publishers.

b) Control and freedom: Different members of a group will have differing needs to control others and to be influential on the decisions relating to goals and activities of the group. In addition, different members of the group at different times will have differing needs for support, help, and direction; people will often want to rely on others to take decisions on their behalf, especially if they are too difficult, confusing, or likely to bring about conflict.

c) Warmth, affection, and intimacy. Different members of the group at different times, and at different times for each individual, will differ in their need to be close with other members of the group. Sometimes there will be a high need for warmth, affection, and intimacy and sometimes there will be a high need for cool, distant, or more formal relationships.

Getting everyone in a team to want the same thing from each other at the same time, or with complimentary needs, is hard; therefore, in any group, the need for understanding and the ability to "read" others is high.

The eternal dilemma that presents itself is that, depending on how each of the group members is hardwired and depending on the day of the week, the pressures on each individual or the group as a whole or even potentially the mood and mindset of the day will have a significant impact on how each group member shows up at any one time. This means that it is almost impossible to reconcile the individual contextual and ever-changing needs of the members of the group, for participation, control, affection, etc., with that of the group. It takes a fair bit of investment from the individuals in a team to take the time and energy to focus on their own needs and the needs of others in their team; therefore, they really have to be able to see the value of investing and need to really care about each other in order to find this energy. However, paradoxically, if the needs in these three categories are not met for a member of the group, much of the energy of the group's members will be diverted to resolving emotional issues, when it is much needed in the space of resolving operational issues.

Some things to observe around interactions of a team:

- Is the leadership directive or inclusive and participative?
- Is the leadership shared between the legitimate leader and others in the group?

- What happens in the group when the leader leads? What do others do?
- Are there clear goals and a clear purpose for the group? Does everyone understand it? Is it agreed to by all?
- Is there any discussion about how to proceed when setting goals or making decisions?
- Is this process directed only by the leader or is there a sharing of the load in a supportive way?
- Does everyone have a chance to participate or are some excluded?
- Do a few dominate the discussion? How are quieter members brought in, if at all?
- Do members have an apparent equality of membership, influence, and belonging or is someone just taking the notes or making the tea?
- Are members appearing to be sensitive and caring towards the needs of other members?
- Do people seem to be feeling that they are being treated well, sensitively, and fairly?
- Do people talk freely or do they seem to stop talking at a certain point?
- Is there an atmosphere?
- Is there interrupting and/or cutting people off?
- Do people really seem to be listening to others, showing that they are hearing what others are saying?
- Is there support and encouragement for ideas, risk taking, failure, and admission of mistakes?
- Is there identification and/or challenge of unacceptable behaviours?

To recap the elements of a well skilled and experienced OD practitioner, as opposed to a workshop facilitator:

Firstly – an OD Practitioner must have a theoretic and practical understanding of the foundations of OD; the main concepts being action research, systems theory, and change theory. Where did OD come from? What are its histories and experiences? Who are the gurus? What do they say? How have all the historical and more recent models been formed? What research has been done? What are the best case studies to refer to? And so on. While we have covered a small amount of that background in this book, there are some epic texts to read to cover the whole subject in much more detail.

Secondly - an OD Practitioner should hold and display the behaviours that show they live by a similar set of values and philosophies. These are how the OD Practitioner shows up in your organisation: their ways of being, how they use themselves as an instrument for change in your organisation, and how they manage their own presence and ego for the good of the system in which they are intervening. The values and philosophies of an OD practitioner are humanistic in their nature, and Gellerman et al.[44] provide a great list, an overview, describing the OD practitioner as having an enthusiastic and committed pursuit of the following:

- Organisations are living systems, so can't be operated like a machine. With certainty, systems can only be disturbed, and our role as OD consultants is to bring something to the system that is missing and usefully disturb the system.

- By bringing as much of the whole system as possible to any given issue, maximum data, understanding co-construction, and ownership can be gained for the required change: "People will support what they help to create"[45].

- A belief that everyone deserves respect, dignity, freedom, justice, and the ability to determine their own future.

- Human potential is unlimited and therefore everyone should have meaningful participation in system affairs, democracy, and appropriate decision making.

- We should be flexible and proactive and seek collaboration through being authentic by displaying congruence, honesty, openness, understanding, and acceptance.

Thirdly - There is a set of ethics that should be present in the client/consultant relationship, so any good OD consultant will be very open about their responsibilities to:

- Their client (mindful of how they represent their skills, the work potentials and risks, and how the client will develop),

44 Gellerman, W., Frankel, M.S. & Ladenson, R.F. (1990). *Values and Ethics in Organization and Human Systems Development: Responding to Dilemmas in Professional Life.* San Francisco: Jossey-Bass.

45 Weisbord, M.R. (1987) *Productive Workplaces, Organizing and Managing for Dignity, Meaning and Community.* San Francisco: Jossey-Bass.

- Themselves (mindful of the need for professional development and working within competence, practicing self-care and containment),
- Their profession (mindful that they represent the whole profession and the need to contribute to the collective understanding of OD),
- Their community (mindful of the wider systemic impacts of any intervention).

There is a whole field of research and many great articles written about "use of self" and "ego" in organisational development consultancy. Mary Ann Rainey and Jonno Hanafin cover this really well, so if you only read one text on this, read their chapter in the NTL handbook[46]. If you have more time, see the life's work of Mee-Yan Cheung Judge in her Global Use of Self Report[47].

The overriding conclusion and the thing to bear in mind at all times is that, as OD practitioners, we must continue to work on our "stuff", maintain rigorous boundaries at all times, and always remember that we are in service of the client and not ourselves.

46 Tolbert, M.A.R. & Hanafin, J. (2006). Use of Self in OD Consulting: What Matters in Presence. Available at: https://maraineyassociates.com/wp-content/uploads/2015/12/UseofSelf-Presence.pdf
47 Cheung-Judge, M.Y. & Jamieson, D.W. (2022). Global Use of Self Research Report. Available at: https://www.quality-equality.com/uosreport

CHAPTER 9

WHY DO WE SPECIALISE IN LEADERS AND THEIR TEAMS?

As organisational development practitioners, there are quite a few directions our practices can take. We can work on the **interpersonal level**, one-to-one on coaching and mentoring and supporting individuals in organisations. Coaching and mentoring individuals at all levels in organisations forms a part of our organisational practice.

We can work on an **intrapersonal level**, supporting the development of excellent relationships between two or three people to ensure operational effectiveness. Our support allows them to get to a place where their relationships need to be, for each of them to be the most effective they can be in their role. This is to ensure that their part of the organisation works exceptionally well because their relationships are strong. We do some of this in the form of mediation or facilitated conversations, but it forms only a small part of our practice.

Zooming out for a moment, we could choose to work at a **whole system level**, depending of course on what you consider the system to be at any one time, as it could be as big as the human race or as small as a chain of location-based subsidiaries of an organisation. However, given that we work almost exclusively in the public sector, our systems are complicated by the political overlay. As the political cycle is three, four, or five years, depending on which location we are operating in and whether it is national politics or local politics, we consider this to be both a hard, impenetrable, and often futile environment for us to seek to work in. Given that many of us have worked at the heart of government for many years, we know only too well the machinations of the electorally sensitive timelines to delivering real and sustainable change. Therefore, while we work in the government sector, it isn't at a system-wide scale by choice.

Over time and with much trial and error about what works and is a satisfying way to make a difference, we have chosen our calling to work with senior leaders in public sector organisations to be the best leaders they can be. They are often beleaguered by the political process, caught in the middle of having to deliver what the politicians want in the electoral cycle and doing the right thing for the long-term sustainability of the system they are the guardians of. Given that we have much experience and bear the scars of political buffering (one too many changes in the machineries of government, delivered at huge cost and with no real need!), we choose to support and work with leaders in the public sector who carry a heavy burden for safe, effective, cost-conscious delivery of often under resourced services to a public whose expectations are always on the increase. For these reasons, this is such a rewarding and challenging environment in which to work.

It is rewarding because just a few small improvements to how leaders leadership teams work in this environment can not only create improvements for whole swathes of public sector staff, but those improvements, when linked to motivation and engagement, are inextricably linked to better outcomes for the public who receive the services. Michael West's research on the NHS[48] shows us the direct correlation between how staff are treated, led, and managed (or, in other words, how they feel valued and engaged) and patient safety and outcomes in public healthcare.

Who wouldn't want to be involved in supporting public sector leaders and their delivery teams to provide excellence to the people they serve, while seeing these outcomes change lives? It is about as rewarding as it gets!

48 West, M.A. Borrill, C. Dawson, J. Scully, J. Carter, M. Anelay, S. Patterson, M. & Waring, J. (2002). *The link between the management of employees and patient mortality in acute hospitals, The International Journal of Human Resource Management, 13*(8), 1299-1310.

PART FOUR
THE SEVEN CLANS
OF LEADERSHIP

Including
"The Spirit of STELLAR"

Introduction to Part 4 - Where does this story fit into a book on developing high performing teams?

We always knew we would come a point when we needed to record the work we had done, the model we had created, the lessons we had learned along the way, and the true magic of using a coaching approach to support teams to create high performance. We always knew there would be a time when we would have the space to write a book. Like most people who work in this field and have ambitions to write a book, the drawbacks are time, space, and trading off working with fee paying clients to invest a huge amount of time away from earning fees to put pen to paper.

Several years ago, we reached an agreement with a UK publisher to write a book on the then called STAR model, but due to the client facing work always taking priority, we never got around to it. On moving to Australia and finding out more about the history and culture of the country here, we began to draw parallels between the connected and holistic nature of the STELLAR MODEL® and the old ways of the indigenous culture, one of the oldest continuous cultures on the planet[49]. It felt respectful, right, and appropriate that, as we began to plan the contents of this work, we collaborated with members of the first people of Australia, as we were writing this on their land. In discussions with Munu (remember we introduced you to Munu in Chapter 2), as he painted his depiction of the STELLAR MODEL®, he talked at length about the seven clans he saw in the model, how they all connected, and how they needed to work together. What follows in Chapter 10 is a fable, a story, written in the style of indigenous storytelling, as we transcribed what we heard when Munu told his story of the Seven Clans through his amazing art and verbal story telling.

In Chapter 11, we explain in a bit more detail the overview of how we apply the STELLAR MODEL® to leaders and their teams in organisations, and then in Chapters 12–19, we unpick each element individually, giving you the insight you need to understand what we mean by "the element", what "good" looks like in organisations, and how you might develop your team or lead the development of a team in this area.

49 Australian Geographic (2022). DNA confirms Aboriginal culture one of Earth's oldest. Available at: https://www.australiangeographic.com.au/news/2011/09/dna-confirms-aboriginal-culture-one-of-earths-oldest/

CHAPTER 10

THE STORY OF "THE SPIRIT OF STELLAR"

Introduction to our ancient tale.

This story was narrated by Munu Wuthuga Dadarkiin when he heard our explanation of the STELLAR MODEL® and what we wanted to do in our support of the development of teams. His interpretation of that was the painting entitled *The Seven Clans*. In this he saw the interconnectedness of all the elements that go together to create a high performing team and re-interpreted this in the story of The Spirit of STELLAR, a character who appears to the elders of a tribe to support them to lead their clans well.

THE SPIRIT OF STELLAR

Once upon a time, in a land not that far away, there was a tribe made up of seven clans who held a central belief that the need for a shared purpose was vital to their sustainability as a tribe. They were very clear that their purpose was to look after the country on which they lived, hunted, and gathered their food (taking only what they needed). They knew that if they fulfilled their purpose, were good guardians of the country, it would continue providing them with what they needed to flourish. If they respected the land, the seasons, the natural resources, the spirits, and the ancient stories of the spirits, who represented all aspects of a connected way of living, then all would be well and the tribe could weather any storm. If they were strong, united, and connected, they would thrive.

This tribe lived as one with the land, with the country. They only felt at home when the land and all it supported worked together well, when all things were in balance. The country provided them with everything they needed: food, shelter, medicine, and, above all, a purpose. All humans need a purpose, a reason for being, and theirs couldn't be clearer. All was well for thousands of years. From time to time, they needed to regroup and remind each other of why their way of life worked, because of their deep respect for the land on which they lived and all the other creatures and vegetation they shared the land with.

When they forgot their purpose and hunted too many animals or harvested berries at the wrong time of year, they were not honouring their purpose and other things started to go wrong. They would begin to lose their way when they lost focus on their purpose. As the clans grew, or new Elders took their place in the leadership of the tribe, if they didn't relay the purpose and the importance of every clan's role in delivering it, or act as good role models for what to do and how to behave, their way of life slowly started to unravel.

For example, there would be differences of opinion or disagreements, but these might not be openly discussed, or some clans would go off and do things their own way, not following the plans, not pursuing a shared purpose that had been agreed about the way the tribe would work as a whole. Or at times, their behaviour to each other would fall below their usual inclusive, compassionate approach. They might find themselves unable to agree about what to do next or what decisions needed making, and because they all didn't agree, some clans would say they would alter where they hunted but then (to protect the people of their own clan and not the tribe as a whole) not really do what they had agreed to. Because they were a proud tribe, they could all see what was going wrong, but no-one was prepared to admit their own part in it, their own fears, and lack of certain skills to turn around the situation.

Fortunately, they had a very wise set of Elders who knew things needed to be brought back on track if the tribe was to survive. They called upon the help of the spirits, asking for advice, support, and wisdom. The spirits told them a story of a mythical creature who was so strong, wise, and healthy that no sickness, battles, or other threats could harm them. This mythical creature was called STELLAR.

STELLAR was created when the planets aligned to produced eight elements, which united to form one strong and invincible force. STELLAR knew everything that needed to be known about how tribes and clans could live together in peace and harmony and how all clans that made up tribes needed to work together as one, to collaborate on the running of the whole tribe.

STELLAR had helped and supported many, many tribes to reach their full potential. The spirits explained that STELLAR would appear to the Elders and teach them ways to support their tribes and the clans by reconnecting to their purpose.

When STELLAR appeared to the Elders, it was a magical night. The sky was clear, there were many stars, and STELLER rose from the river with such force that the Elders were afraid at first. But, remembering what the spirits had told them, remembering the power of STELLAR, they faced their fears and waited for STELLAR to teach them some new ways to work well with their tribe.

STELLAR's voice was strong and clear as they began to explain the eight elements from which they were made, beginning with ***PURPOSEFULLY***. STELLAR explained that tribes who knew their purpose, celebrated their purpose, reviewed it to make sure it was still relevant, and allowed every member of the tribe to talk about what it meant to live their lives ***PURPOSEFULLY***. All creatures, including humans, across all lands needed to know what their purpose was and the role they fulfilled as individuals and together in their herds, packs, or tribes; once we knew this purpose and lived our lives to deliver it, we felt complete, we had a purpose, we were living ***PURPOSEFULLY***.

The tribe needed to live PURPOSEFULLY

Figure 19: Icon of STELLAR MODEL® Element PURPOSEFULLY, depicting the indigenous symbol for running water

STELLAR then told stories to the tribespeople about how beautiful the future would be when they all worked together, creating a powerful and easily understood vision of the future. It wasn't STELLAR's job to tell the Elders what the vision should be; they had to create this together with all members of the tribe, as when people create something together, they all have an interest in making it happen. It was STELLAR's job to make sure the Elders understood the importance of having a vision and involving people in creating it. Once the Elders had worked with all their people to create a vision, this picture they created together would become a guiding force to propel the tribe forward in one direction to deliver that vision. The direction would be their metaphorical journey as a tribe, and as long as they could break this journey down into smaller steps, or in reality, into tasks for each member of the clan or tribe, they would have a practical way of making sure the vision was delivered.

Therefore, by creating a vision, having that destination and journey, and by breaking it down into smaller, achievable steps or tasks, there was a very good chance that the tribe would get as close as they could to bringing their vision to life; this would mean they were delivering their purpose ***STRATEGICALLY***.

The tribe needed to live STRATEGICALLY

Figure 20: Icon of STELLAR MODEL® element Strategically, depicting a number
of people meeting and seeking the input of others on their planning

STELLAR also knew that reaching this vision and keeping their focus in the longer term, while striving to get the in-the-moment tasks done, for any tribe, would never be without its trials and tribulations.

Things happen even in the most well led tribe, to anyone and anywhere at any time that can't be predicted. The possibility of invasions, sickness, other tribes developing differently, and an endless list of everything that could go wrong was ever present. Knowing that unexpected difficulties could crop up at any time, STELLAR wanted the tribe to understand that how they made decisions about all the big and small things was a skill; a skill that needed to be worked on and practiced so that the tribe would be able to make the right decisions, or at least make the best decision they could in the circumstances, rather than drifting through each day, letting outside influences decide how they lived.

Making no decision at all or deciding then not acting is one of the easiest ways to lead a tribe into disarray. STELLAR agreed to work with the tribe to help them learn how best to make and enact their decisions so that everyone in the tribe knew what the decisions were, what the way forward was, and how they needed to act to make sure the decision was put in place. This, STELLAR explained, would enable the tribe to deliver their purpose and achieve their strategic, long-term vision **DECISIVELY**.

The tribe needed to live DECISIVELY

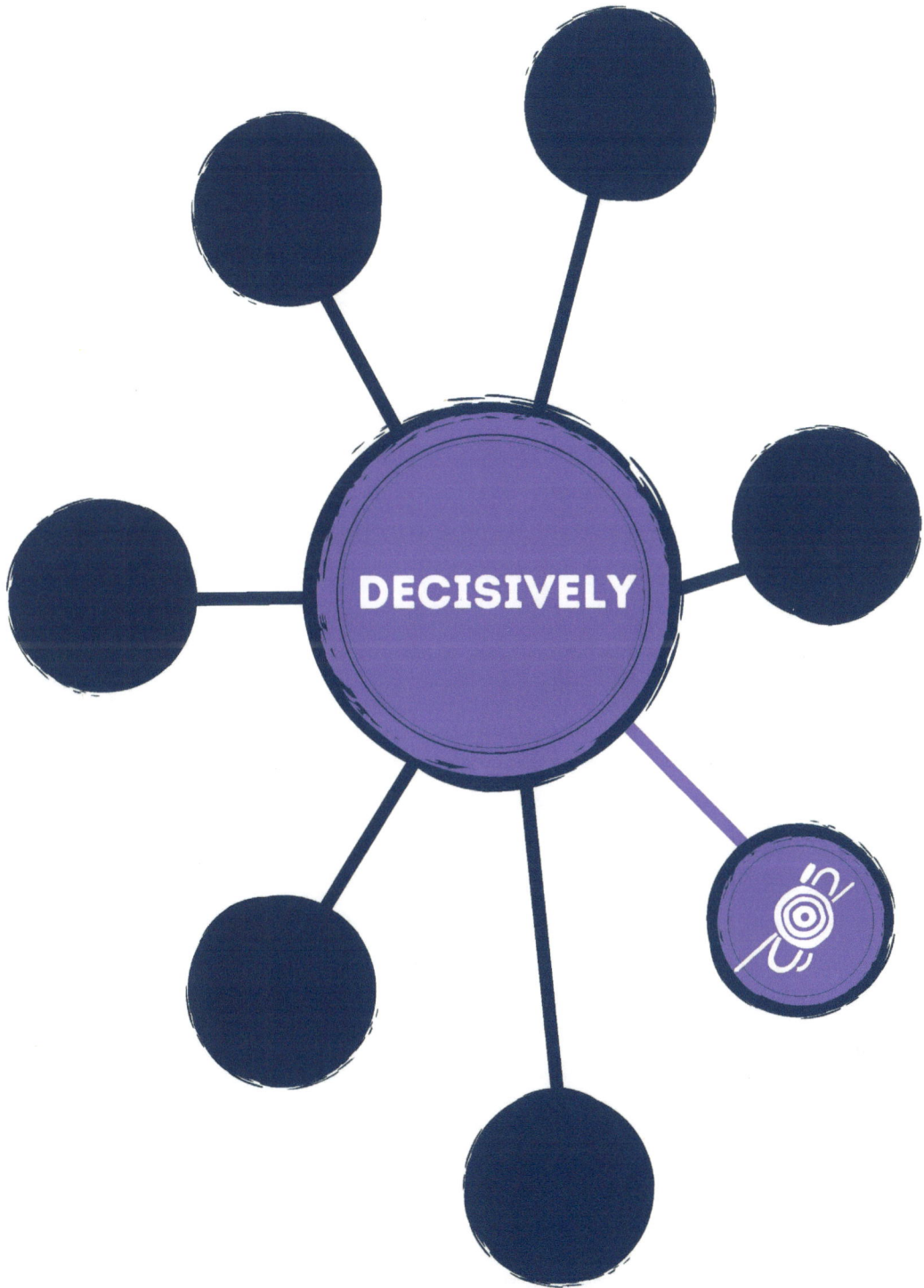

Figure 21: Icon from the STELLAR MODEL® element Decisively, depicting
two people meeting with a spear, boomerang, digging stick, and
coolamon (vessel for carrying babies or water), making decisions

The next step was to make sure that everyone in the tribe knew their personal role in making all the decisions happen, making sure the direction they were individually heading in, the actions they were taking each day to deliver the tasks, were the right ones, done in the right way, and having the right impact to be effective at delivering their plans, their vision, and their purpose. But how did the Elders know this was happening across the whole tribe? The Elders were the ones meeting each day, painting the vision for the future, but they weren't at the head of the hunting party each morning to know where the hunt was going, what they were hunting for, and, for every spear they used, how many animals they were able to hunt. STELLAR told them that the most successful tribes listened to all its tribespeople, worked with the leaders of each clan, and made sure that involvement in the way things worked spread across the whole tribe.

They made sure to spread the listening and involvement of everyone across the whole tribe by having the tribe's Elders, and the leaders at all levels of the tribe and each clan, the hunting party leaders for example, come together regularly. They would talk about what they had been doing, get an update from each other about what was going on, and share what they had been doing to deliver the tasks, and thus they got updates about the impact of external forces on the tribe so that they could modify the tasks if needed.

It also required everyone in the tribe to make a commitment about what they were going to do that day or that week and to live up to that commitment. If they couldn't do what they had promised or they made a mistake, they all agreed that they would speak up and ask for help from the wider clan to help them deliver. Saying what you are going to do, then doing what you said you were going to do, STELLAR called living **ACCOUNTABLY**.

The tribe needed to live ACCOUNTABLY

Figure 22: Icon from the STELLAR MODEL® element Accountably, depicting two very important people meeting with a hunting boomerang and a spear, agreeing their roles in the tribe

Up to this point, STELLAR appeared to have only spoken about the work the tribe had to do to move forward and thrive. STELLAR explained that if everyone did as they had said, then the tribe would thrive, or at least appear to thrive. However, STELLAR urged caution when thinking this would last. It would last for a time, but people living and working together needed more than direction or a straight path to follow. They also needed love, compassion, kindness, and the safety of their fellow tribespeople; a certainty that the people around them cared for their wellbeing. There were four more important things STELLAR had to teach this tribe: the elements of how to live in harmony with each other.

The first part of the wisdom from STELLAR (the first four elements) explained how important it was to have a clear purpose and set a clear direction with the creation of a pathway to deliver the vision, having everyone being accountable for their actions and making good decisions. The remaining four elements all supported how they may live together harmoniously. People will want to follow Elders if they trust them, and trust wasn't something that STELLAR could give to the tribe. Trust is easily lost when people in a tribe aren't treated well. How the Elders behaved, how each person in the tribe treated each other, was vital to sustain a flourishing tribe. What STELLAR had seen in other places was that, even in times of great strain and suffering, tribespeople would do more, be more, and achieve more when living in a place that nurtured them, that cared for them, that wanted the best for them and showed them that they were valued and respected. This started by setting some clear expectations, being clear about the roles and responsibilities that all members of the tribe should live up to and had to be accountable for. They also needed to give clear and kind feedback about how everyone was doing, whether they were meeting the agreements they had made about what they would do, and then offering support to each other to help them learn what they needed to learn and develop into what they needed to develop into to be the person the tribe needed them to be for the tribe to flourish. This was called living **CLEARLY**.

The tribe needed to live CLEARLY

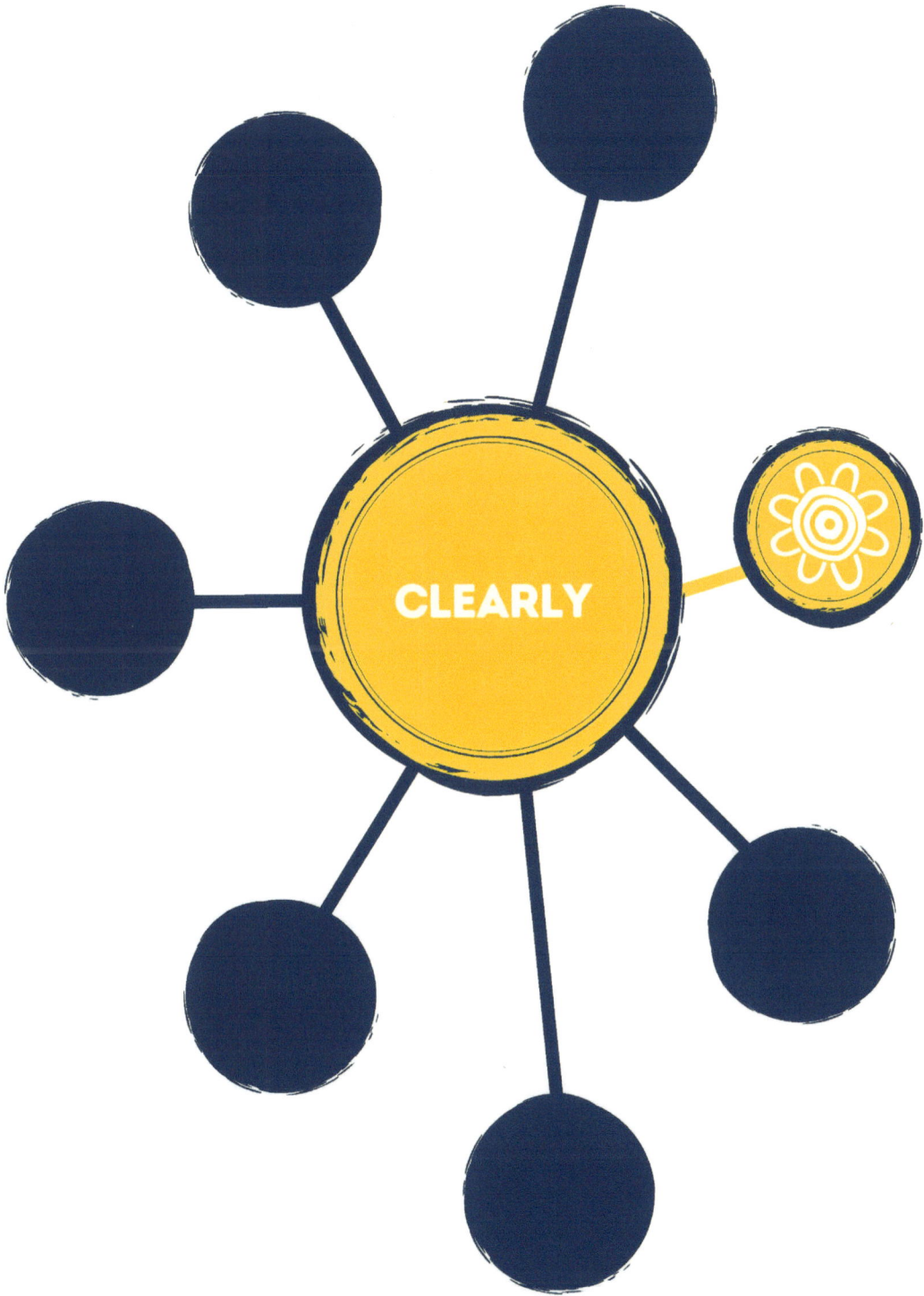

Figure 23: Icon from the STELLAR MODEL® element Clearly, depicting a number of people in meetings being clear with each other in their discussions and expectations

There was a clarity also needed across the members of the tribe about behaviours, what was and wasn't acceptable, something which needed discussing and agreeing, firstly amongst the Elders then across the whole tribe.

However, they described the behaviours they expected from each other, and they all stemmed from the simple description of living **KINDLY**.

Every tribe, every group of people living in their different settings, will find different behaviours acceptable and unacceptable. Therefore, it is important for each tribe to work on their own list of such behaviours, and when they have an agreed list for everyone, they must openly agree to that list and want to be held accountable for living up to the behaviours they have agreed to. They will then be able to challenge each other when they don't live up to these, while supporting them to do better, to be better.

The tribe needed to live KINDLY

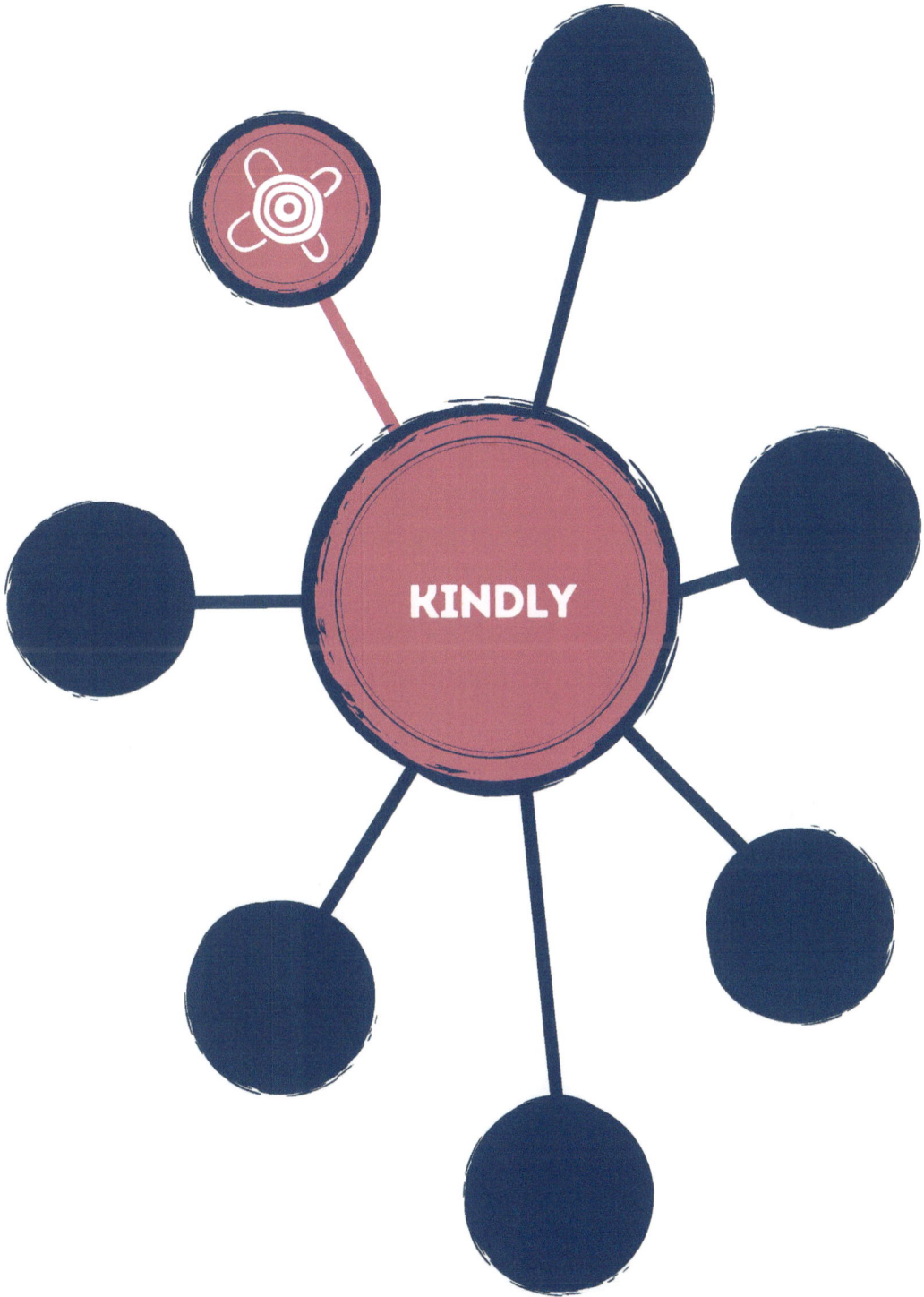

Figure 24: Icon from the STELLAR MODEL® element Kindly,
depicting four people meeting to support each other

STELLAR explained that sometimes the relationships we have with people don't always go smoothly. We are all different, even if we have lived in the same place with the same people all our lives.

Some of us talk a lot, others need quiet.

Some of us share a lot about ourselves and want to know everything about everyone, and some of us are more contained.

Some of us focus on the detail, the next step, and the next step after that, and some of us focus on the big picture, the whole. Most of us dip in and out of being some or all the above, depending on what is happening in our lives and what is happening with the pressures of delivering what we need to do in our work to support our tribe being successful.

The amount of inclusion, control, and affection that we need and are prepared to give to others supports the strength and quality of our relation-ships. Plus, there are those little things, which can become big things, that wind us up about how others do their thing. It could be tardiness, words or phrases people use, what we perceive to be their commitment to delivering their role, our perception of how much they care, or their effort, for example.

STELLAR wisely reminded the Elders that sometimes the things that hook into us about other people are the things we least like about ourselves, so if we are always wound up by our perceptions of others' incompetence or commitment, it may because we are secretly afraid that others think we are not competent or committed.

Therefore, STELLAR made sure the Elders understood that it was very important to know that conflict, disagreements, and misunderstandings would always happen in any tribe or clan, no matter how well they were doing everything. It was crucial that everyone in the tribe knew how to deal with this when it arose.

STELLAR had seen many tribes often ignore issues that needed dealing with. They seemed to think that it was kinder and easier to ignore issues or deliberately push difficult things that needed dealing with "under the ground" so that people didn't get upset or so that the group didn't fracture or need to deal with things that were too hard for them to deal with alone. However, this wasn't kind or easier in the long run. What happened was that the pile of things "under the ground" got bigger and bigger, and at some point, it just couldn't be ignored any more.

These issues grew and grew if they weren't dealt with, and what might have started as a small issue (for example about how someone phrased something or interrupted someone), if not challenged, would be repeated time and time again, and the feelings of those who were offended would grow and grow, until one day, there would be a last straw and the issue that had started so small would explode. Someone would shout or cry or leave the tribe after having landed their unhappiness or anger in the middle of a meeting place, leaving everyone who was there to soak up the heat of the emotion.

STELLAR explained to the Elders that it didn't need to be like that. If people embraced the difference in the tribe, acknowledged that all people behaved differently, had different experiences and skills, and saw the beauty of that difference and diversity, they could bring their differences together to use them for the good of the tribe. The differences would allow them to be more creative, more inventive about ways to do things that helped the tribe thrive.

This meant that for most members of the tribe, there was some work to do on learning skills that they had perhaps not learned from their upbringing. Depending on how they were raised, in a proud people who saw strength as being able to put up with things, it was likely that they may avoid conflict and not see the beauty in it.

STELLAR wanted them to learn how to embrace difference and the good that might come from the possible conflict. STELLAR was letting them know that they had to be open to the power of curiosity and wanted them to be curious about why they reacted to others in the way they did. What was it in their past that caused the behaviour to hook into them in some way to push their "hot buttons"? Did they see something in the other person that they perhaps consciously or subconsciously didn't quite like about themselves? Or was the other person displaying behaviours that had caused issues or unpleasantness in the past?

STELLAR wanted them to be curious about other people in the tribe. What was it about their past experiences, how they were "hard wired"? What was going on for them at that moment in their lives that caused them to show up in that way, behave in that way? Often, when conflict or disagreements happen and people begin to discuss it, some sense of defensiveness can arise. STELLAR reminded the Elders that most people were doing their best and were using the skills they had, even if we judged those skills to not be enough or even to be unhelpful. Therefore, if everyone tried their best to be curious, it would be really hard to be defensive at the same time; the two don't work too well together, so getting better at curiosity would help stave off any really serious conflict before it had begun.

STELLAR wanted them to be curious about the clan, the tribe, and the whole country and eco-system in which they operated. This was because every edge that was placed on an organism, every boundary, real or imagined, created tension of some sort. Once people bumped up against other views in their tribe, or even the imaginary boundary they had created for themselves, they reacted. It was due to cause and effect, action, and reaction.

This curiosity, coupled with asking some kind and supportive questions, and a commitment from everyone in the tribe to stay with the moment of conflict and sort it out, even when it was a small issue, and to stop ignoring things, would support the tribe to thrive, even when there were disagreements, conflicts, and even all-out battle.

The tribe needed to live curiously

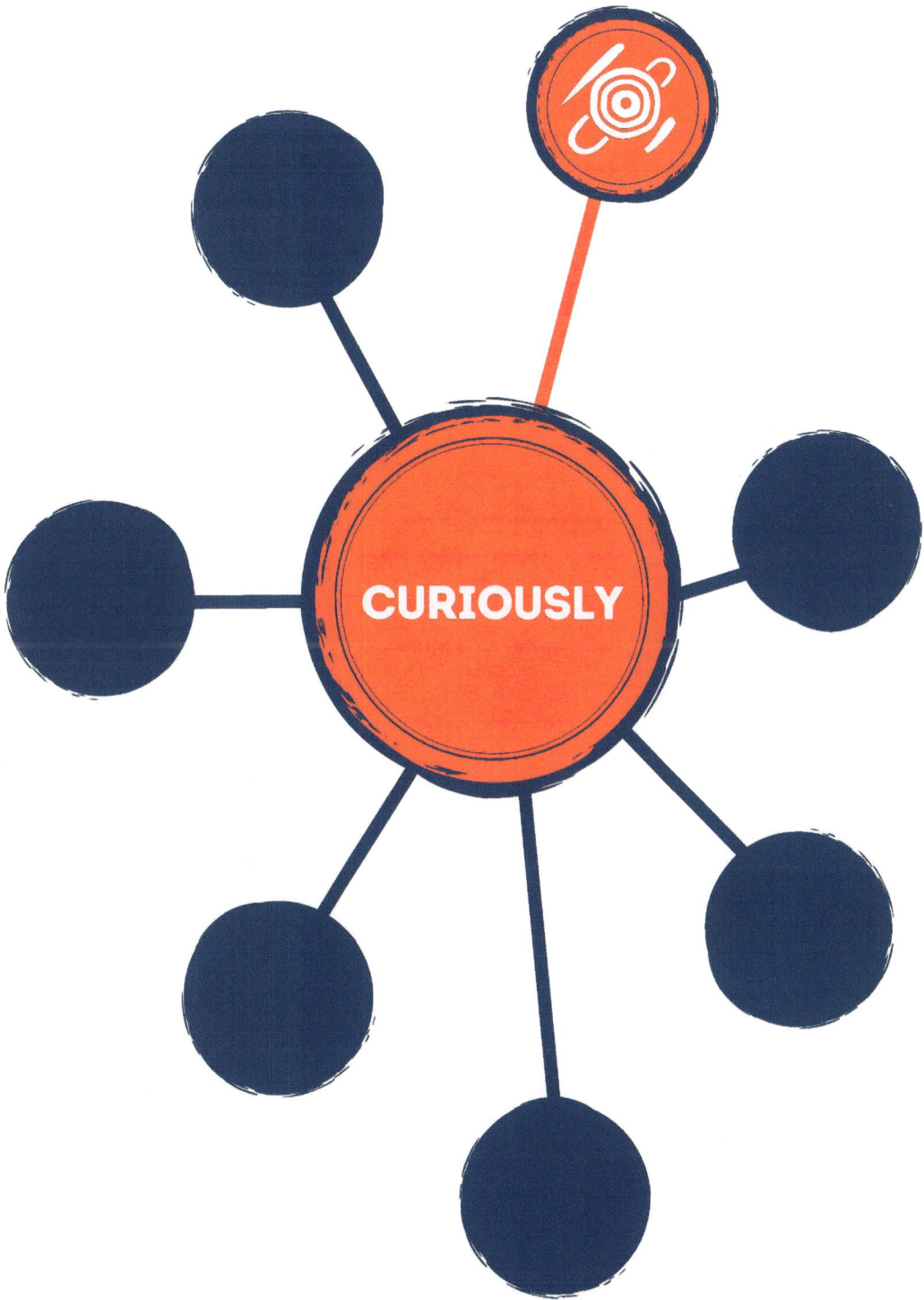

Figure 25: Icon from the STELLAR MODEL® element Curiously, depicting two people asking each other questions; one holding a digging stick and one holding a coolamon

Finally, STELLAR was clear with the Elders that they, more than anyone else in the tribe, needed to set a good example by not pretending that they knew all the answers. They were a proud people; the Elders were in their positions because they had lived a long time, seen a lot of things over the years, and had lots of life experience. But no matter how much they knew, how much they thought they were supposed to know to live up to the faith that the people of the tribe had in them, they would never, ever know everything or have all the answers.

STELLAR wanted them to make sure that all the people in the tribe knew that the Elders were open to hearing the answers and solutions from the tribespeople and that the Elders were in their positions because they were brave enough to say they that didn't know everything and knew when it was right to ask for help. This had many benefits.

The Elders began to shake off their fears of needing to always look invincible and started to show their people how to ask for help. This set a good example to everyone in the tribe, showing that admitting you needed help, telling people you had made a mistake, and asking for support, or letting people know you didn't know what to do next, was brave, courageous, and strong.

This had a great impact and began to cause others, who might have muddled through, kept their worries to themselves, or covered up their mistakes, to bring things out into the open, seek help, admit they were struggling, and be brave enough to declare that they needed support. What STELLAR wanted was the tribe, and particularly the Elders, to show vulnerability.

STELLAR knew this might be hardest of all because, for many of the tribespeople, particularly the Elders and other leaders, they had been told from the beginning of their lives that they needed to be strong, needed to stop crying, needed to grow up and be independent. What they failed to understand is that the basic need for all humans in whatever culture or tribe they come from is connection and trust. We can only trust people who show us enough of their real selves so that we can find some similarities, some connection. Many of the Elders had become so removed from the people in the tribe who did the day-to-day work that they felt no connection to the Elders and therefore found it hard to trust them. If the Elders were able to gain the trust of the whole tribe by showing vulnerability, then this would allow the tribe to thrive in the long term.

The tribe needed to live VULNERABLY

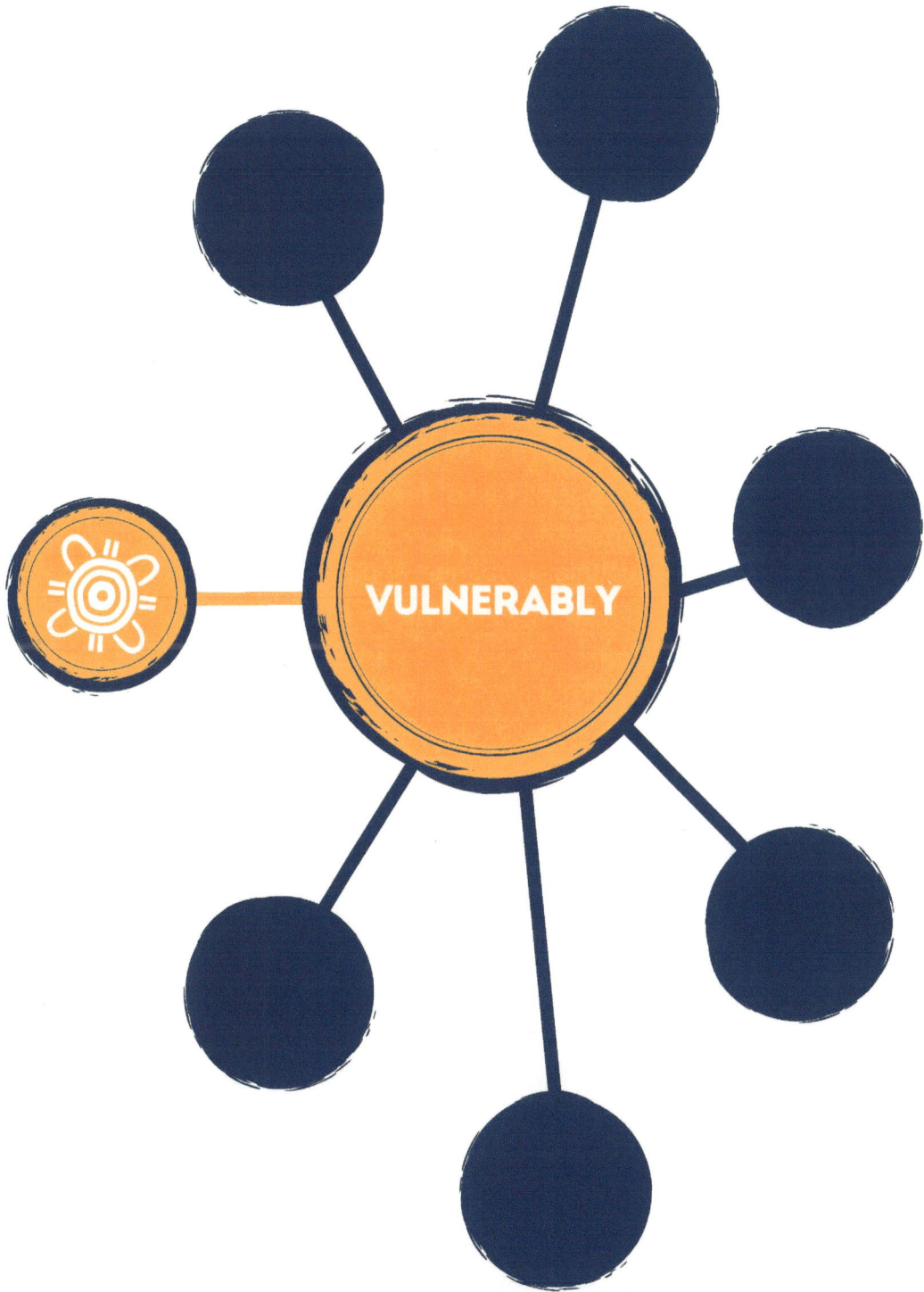

Figure 26: Icon from the STELLAR MODEL® element Vulnerably, depicting four people speaking with their message/clapping sticks laid down on the floor

The Elders listened to the wisdom of STELLAR and put in place some of the teachings, and they talked with the wider group of leaders to make sure everyone agreed that they would put in place their plan for the tribes to thrive.

The Elders arranged many days of whole tribe meetings, celebrating how much they had learned and sharing stories with each other of how each clan had progressed.

The Elders explained what they had learned from STELLAR and how all tribes and clans needed to keep working on themselves, on the work they did together, and how they did that work. The tribe was now going to move on from having fallen into a pattern of living alongside each other as a co-existing group but not really living as an interdependent tribe. This had stopped them, for a time, living up to the responsibilities of being guardians of the country in which they lived, of living up to their purpose. The Elders were clear with the whole tribe that this was going to change, and if the Elders themselves could be brave enough to seek out and accept the help of STELLAR, then they expected the whole tribe to work together to improve the tribe for the good of the country, the good of the tribe, and the good of every individual.

The Elders told the story of how STELLAR had come to talk to them after they had asked the spirits for help. STELLAR had explained the eight things that needed to be in place to make sure the tribe thrived. Everyone was captivated by the stories and could see the wisdom in STELLAR's words and experience. The first thing they decided to do in their whole tribe meeting was discuss their purpose as a tribe.

This took a long time; not because they disagreed on the fundamentals but because they wanted to make sure that everyone's way of describing the purpose was honoured. Each person either needs to see their words in a purpose statement or be able to accept, understand, and happily use others' words because they can recognise their proximity to the words they would have wanted to be used.

There was a lot of discussion, some disagreement, and some evidence that they still had work to do on living kindly, but the Elders remembered STELLAR's advice: "Trust in the process, your tribe is wise, and with the right support, challenges, and intervention, your tribe will heal itself."

After much debate and much rewriting, they all agreed the wording would be:

Our purpose is to be the guardians of the country in which we live, hunt, and harvest and to protect our country so that our tribe is sustainable and our country flourishes.

The agreement was reached that this was the purpose of the tribe and to live in a way that supported the delivery of the purpose was to live **PURPOSEFULLY**.

The Elders asked each of the clans to take ownership of one of the remaining seven elements that STELLAR had taught them, and the Elders themselves would take ownership of tending to the purpose of the tribe.

So, each of the clans made a case to the Elders and the other clans for the guardianship of the lesson that they felt most able to tend for the benefit of the whole tribe.

When each of the elements had its owning clan, they spent some time with an elder who made sure they really understood the teachings of STELLAR. They could then craft the ways in which they would tend to the element and the ways they would work with the other clans. At the end of the big tribe meetings, they all made sure everyone understood how they needed to behave and what they needed to do together to enable the tribe to thrive.

Magical, mythical tales like this might usually end with "and they all lived happily ever after". That is not the case here and is not usually the case anywhere when we are talking about how people behave. As STELLAR had rightly predicted, things happen in any tribe or clan that presents everyone who is part of a tribe with problems to overcome. The world keeps turning and throwing up new and interesting issues every day, every week, every year. The only certain thing is that this will keep happening.

This tribe knew that they must keep working on the elements, keep talking to each other and planning together, and keep true to their tribe's purpose, sticking to their values. This regular attention to what they did as a tribe and how they behaved as a people would ensure that they could see through any hardships that befell them.

There were many hardships, but each year, STELLAR came back to the Elders to provide ongoing support and teach them new ways to keep working on the tribe. If they had stopped paying attention to one or more of the elements, STELLAR would challenge them to do better and support them in equal measure, making sure that the tribe was on the right path and all the tribespeople's hearts were being tended to ensure they all kept developing, moving forward, and thriving as a tribe.

THE STELLAR MODEL®

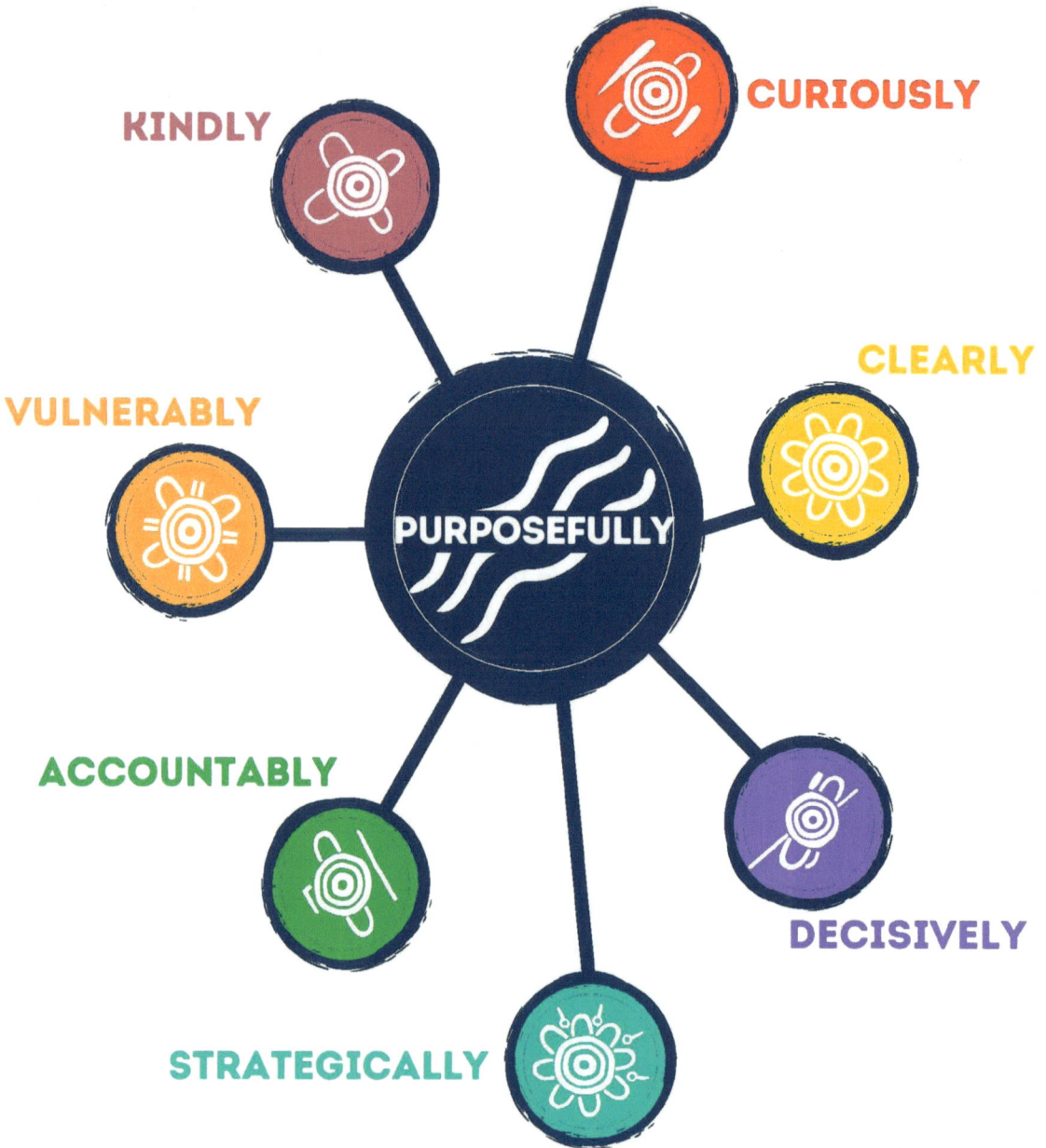

Figure 27 - The STELLAR MODEL® with icons and element names, 2022

CHAPTER 11

HOW WE APPLY THE STELLAR MODEL®

When we work with teams (although it should be said and often repeated that this model works just as well when assessing your own personal leadership approach and style), it is important to find out where they are starting from. Then we offer some suggestions about what the team might do, support them to do that, then show them how far they have moved. We do this by getting a baseline at the start (data gathering, analysis, and feedback), which also uncovers the breadth and depth of the work they need to do. We then usually re-run some of the tests we used to gather the data, which forms the baseline at the end, to show them how far they have come in the time we have worked together.

In **Part 3, Organisational Development - What's That About Then?**, we took you through our eight phases of the OD cycle, explained what they meant and, to some extent, what we do at each stage of that OD cycle. In the remaining chapters of this section, Chapters 12 to 19, we explain each of the elements of the STELLAR MODEL® and relate it to the story of the tribe. We **DEFINE** the element and **EXPLAIN** what this might look like as the best performing team and what we are looking for when we gather our data. We then give you insight into what happens, what tools or techniques we use when we **INTERVENE** with teams, leaving you with some questions, tips, and tools that you might want to think about using. As you read through the next eight chapters, we would like you to keep in mind the following questions to help you assess how mature your team is when benchmarked against the STELLAR MODEL®.

When you stand back and look at all eight elements of the model:

- Are you a team or a group of individual leaders?
- Do you need to be a team? Is it worth the hard work to reap the rewards?
- What example do you want to set for the way others around you work?
- Are you personally able to be vulnerable, kind, and curious?

- Are you clear with others and do you notice and name issues within the team, for the good of the team?

Once you get into the individual elements later in this section and review the more detailed questions under each element, it will be tempting to focus on the elements that you think need the most work. We implore you to also stand back and look at the whole model. Remember, when the clans moved on their own, they put the whole tribe out of sync and they put the tribe at risk. This model should be viewed as a whole; all elements are connected to one another, none more important than the other, none to be ignored or left alone.

It is true that all leaders and leadership teams are stronger in one area than the other, and this will become apparent during the data gathering phase of any work in a client system. They will also be weaker in some areas, so the weaker areas might be a priority for the work to begin. However, to revisit our analogy of the team as a car and working with a team as a car service: just as a mechanic would run through all mechanical, electrical, and bodywork items in a car service, they won't just focus on where the knocking is coming from, they will also change the oil, so the engine keeps running smoothly, even if the oil light is not on. So too, an OD practitioner must complete the client system diagnostic, and even if there is nothing noticeably amiss with one part of the system, it will still be given some attention to allow the whole system to keep running well. We might also pick out some high scoring areas to a) celebrate what is really working well and b) seek to use some Appreciate Inquiry methods to copy any approaches that allow this area to work well and transfer them across to other not so highly scoring elements.

How do we find out how the team or group is currently functioning?

As we have made reference to before, we go through the entry, contracting, data gathering and analysis, feedback, and action planning phases before we get in the room with the whole team. As well as a 1:1 interview and an individual and team psychometric (the latter of which is helpful but not obligatory), we get the individuals to complete our STELLAR MODEL® questionnaire. This is now online, and the scoring outcomes link directly to a plot point on our STELLAR MODEL® MATURITY MATRIX. This means that, for each question, each element, and the whole model, teams can see their outcomes and see whether they are showing up as **Not There Yet, Work in Progress**, or **All Working Well** on any of these elements and what that means in practice.

How does the scoring and plotting on the Maturity Matrix work?

When someone answers one of the questions (there are 16, two for each element), this generates a score, as follows:

- Not There Yet – scores 1
- Work in Progress – scores 2
- All Working Well – scores 3

If someone answered All Working Well for each of the 16 questions, their score would be 48, and this would mean that, in their view, the whole team is All Working Well.

However, if a different person scored everything as Not There Yet, their score would only be 16. If person three did a mix across all three categories, they might come out with a score of 32, depending on what they answered to each question.

When individuals do our online questionnaire, we create cut-off points as percentages to allow everyone to get a report on how they scored overall and by element. When we work with teams, we combine everyone's scores in the team to come up with a whole team view. We add together individual scores for each question, then average it (by dividing it by the number of respondents) and use a normal distribution curve approach to say that any question with an average score of 1-1.5 is Not There Yet, 1.75 – 2.25 is Work in Progress, and 2.5 – 3 is All Working Well. See the example in Figure 28 (over page) where there were four respondents.

In narrative terms, it is helpful for teams to understand what the three categories mean, so we created the maturity matrix, which is a commonly used tool we have adopted to describe the level of maturity or development of a team or organisation[50].

For example, for the central element of **PURPOSEFULLY**, the three categories are described as:

Not There Yet

Can't clearly explain the purpose of this team and how it might be different to the delivery of the work of the team or the organisation. Struggles to see how the vision drives decision-making and action; vision isn't clear or shared amongst the team.

50 Wysocki, R.K. (2004). Project Management Process Improvement. London: Artech House.

RESPONSE 1	RESPONSE 2	RESPONSE 3	RESPONSE 4	TOTAL	AVERAGE
1	1	1	1	4	1
1	1	1	2	5	1.25
1	1	2	2	6	1.5
1	1	1	3	6	1.5
1	2	2	2	7	1.75
1	1	2	3	7	1.75
1	2	2	3	8	2
1	1	3	3	8	2
2	2	2	2	8	2
1	2	3	3	9	2.25
2	2	2	3	9	2.25
1	3	3	3	10	2.5
2	2	3	3	10	2.5
2	3	3	3	11	2.75
3	3	3	3	12	3

NOT THERE YET	WORK IN PROGRESS	ALL WORKING WELL

Figure 28 - Example of scoring for maturity matrix

Work in Progress

Purpose is due for a review to determine if the team is still in alignment; the team is clear about the direction but needs greater integration/cohesion; the purpose doesn't consistently drive decision making.

All Working Well

Team can clearly identify where the purpose has an effect on output, e.g., decision-making implementation, etc. Team purpose creates a passion in the team members; it is a unifying force to align differences and is underpinned by team and organisational values.

You can see our full version of the maturity matrix in Figures 29 and 30. Later on, we have included the detail of the matrix and the scoring system that we use and all the questions in each of the sections.

We share this so you can use them, create your own, or just understand the concept and at the very least give data gathering a go in your own team.

A note of caution: our approach and questions have been built up over many years of trial and error and have now been verified by our organisational psychologist as valid, in terms of input, outcomes, and norms, etc. The way questions are asked, the types of questions you ask, and even the tools you use can skew your outcomes, so while you might want to have a go, and that is great, make sure you have a plan and know what you are trying to discover, and also feel free to use our questions, we know they work!

THE STELLAR MODEL®
TEAM MATURITY MATRIX

 **PURPOSEFULLY**

 **STRATEGICALLY**

 **DECISIVELY**

 **ACCOUNTABLY**

	PURPOSEFULLY	STRATEGICALLY	DECISIVELY	ACCOUNTABLY
NOT THERE YET	People can't clearly explain the purpose of the team and how it might be different to the delivery of the work of the team or the organisation. People struggle to see how the vision drives decision making and action. The vision isn't clear or shared amongst the team.	There are gaps in linking the vision to execution, accountability and ownership. Or there is no current strategy or plan in place to guide activities.	Decisions are not made at all or as a whole team. There is a lack of clarity around what actions need to be taken and communication of decisions is poor or inconsistent.	There is a lack of clarity on performance indicators. People are unclear what others' KPIs are. There is limited discussion around performance beyond immediate deliverables. People aren't held to account; if this is attempted, it is taken personally.
WORK IN PROGRESS	The team purpose is due for a review to determine if the team is still in alignment. People are clear about the direction but greater integration and cohesion is needed. The purpose doesn't consistently drive decision making.	The dots need to be connected between the vision, strategy and execution. The team are working towards clarity on the vision. Effective processes need to be established to clearly link each person's role to team, and organisational goals.	Reaching decisions can take some work with various opinions and perspective competing for agreement. Decisions can sometimes be affected by outside influences. The gaps or overlaps between teams are unclear which makes specific actions tricky to allocate with clarity.	KPIs need to be reviewed to ensure they are still fit for purpose. There is a variable knowledge of others' KPIs and deliverables. Methods for holding one another to account could be improved and clarified.
ALL WORKING WELL	The team can clearly identify where the purpose has an effect on output, e.g. decision making implementation etc. The team purpose creates a passion in the team members, it is a unifying force to align differences and is underpinned by team and organisational values.	The team are clear on their strategic and operational plans. They can all see how their individual efforts impact on the team and the organisation, and vice versa.	The team operates with empowered decision making and with high levels of mutual supportiveness. Everyone is kept informed and is clear on the steps to take and who is taking them.	The team are clear about what their individual KPIs and deliverables are, and how they interact with others' KPIs. This knowledge means everyone can be held to account appropriately, with support and challenge. This isn't taken personally.

Figure 29: Part 1 of the STELLAR MODEL® Maturity Matrix

CLEARLY	KINDLY	CURIOUSLY	VULNERABLY	
Feedback is not given in a timely and respectful manner, or when given it is taken personally. There is little clarity about role boundaries and who or which team is responsible for what. Low levels of team and wider communication and engagement.	A formal behaviour "code" has not been established. Unacceptable behaviours are not challenged There are low levels of psychological safety. There are some factions or cliques within the team.	Perceptions of power make it difficult for others to speak up and challenge. Sayings like "it's just how we do things around here" are frequently used and this stifles discussions around challenging the status quo or challenging those in power. Diversity of thought and experience is not welcome and often "shut down".	Low level of trust and respect throughout the team. People value individual achievement and self-promotion over team results. Functions are siloed and mistakes or difficulties are hidden.	**NOT THERE YET**
Comfort with, feedback being given or received (and how) varies within the group. There could be more clarity about roles and more communication to wider team members and within the team.	The code of behaviour needs reviewing to ensure new team members are included and inducted. Relationships still need to be cultivated amongst the team. There is some psychological safety.	Some things should be brought to light earlier. Some things are left undiscussed to minimise conflict. There are times when some might not feel comfortable speaking up. Some things need to be handled with greater tact.	There is a good acknowledgement of interdependencies but not enough time to appreciate and celebrate achievements. Trust levels are still being cultivated with some trusted more than others. Some are not considered "team players". Errors are reported, but blame shifting might still occur.	**WORK IN PROGRESS**
There are competent skills and a positive mindset around giving and receiving feedback. There is clarity about roles, about who is responsible for what and there is clear communication and engagement within the team and beyond.	There is an authentic desire within the team to provide support and help each other's grow as leaders and individuals. Codes of behaviour are established and adhered to, people easily speak up and apologise.	The team welcomes diversity of thought, experience and approach knowing this brings more creative solutions. The team feels comfortable to "call out" situations early and has the skills to discuss them constructively and reach future focused conclusions.	High levels of mutual respect and trust throughout the team. The delivery of team or organisational goals is placed above individual achievements. People easily ask for help or hold up their hands to admit errors and ask for support.	**ALL WORKING WELL**

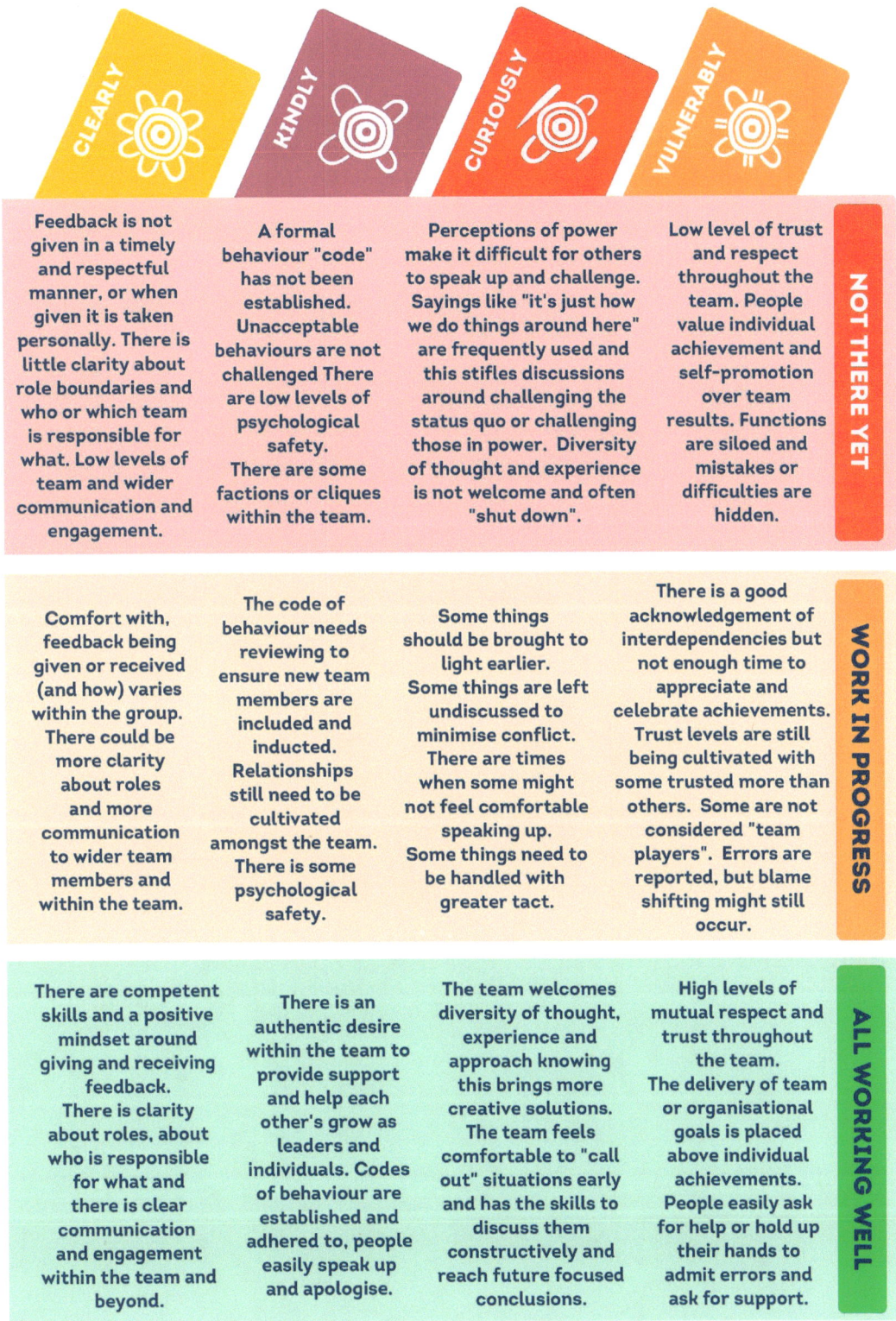

Figure 30: Part 2 of the STELLAR MODEL® Maturity Matrix

We are amassing a lot of data from an array of leaders who have already responded to our questionnaire, and we would love to add to that, so if you choose to use these questions, please share your findings with us so we can keep adding to the growing body of data sets we are collecting for our research in this area. If you want to make it easy for yourself, use the QR code in Figure 31 and complete our two-minute questionnaire. A short report will be sent to you about your own responses and will give you a good indication of where your team sits on the STELLAR TEAM® Maturity Matrix, based on your view. If you want to get the views of the whole team and a collated report, then get in touch with us. The QR code takes you to a landing page. Fill in your information to gain access to complete the questionnaire (the scorecard). Have fun!

Figure 31: STELLAR MODEL® Maturity Matrix questionnaire, via our website

A small aside on the difference between teams and groups

As you look at your team and seek to answer some of the simple questions we posed earlier, it is probably worth trying to put some definitions around when a team is a team or just a group and when a group of people needs to try to be a team.

The best work in this field is by Katzenbatch and Smith[51]. The three biggest differences between teams and groups is the focus on goals, accountability, and outcomes.

Groups tend to be a collection of people who come together to coordinate their efforts, while a team of people tend to share a common purpose.:

- Groups = individual goals, individual accountability, and individual success or failure.

- Teams = shared goals, individual and shared accountability, and collective success.

It is quite important to find out when working with a new client whether or not the people you are working with:

a) Understand this difference,

b) Know whether they are a team at the moment (or should be),

c) Know whether they need to be a team,

d) Are all up for the changes and the effort it will take to become a team and sustain themselves as a high functioning team.

You might put a lot of effort into supporting them to become a team when they don't want to be or don't need to be, so it is worth posing the question.

This is because all the elements of the STELLAR MODEL® take effort, input, and energy to sustain them. If there is no real need for a team to be in place, the OD practitioner's and the client's system efforts might all be either wasted or pointed in the wrong direction.

However, each of the elements of the STELLAR MODEL® do support the functioning of groups as well, and for total transparency, it is important for us to state that we see the benefits of all groups seeking to become a team if they are prepared to put in the effort to get there. The rewards will

---

51 Katzenbatch, J.R., & Smith, D.K. (1993). The Wisdom of Teams: Creating the High-Performance Organization. McKinsey & Company.

be worth it. The downside of staying as a functioning group is that the individual approach doesn't really support intra-organisational goal delivery, as this usually needs some level of collaboration across departments by several members of a team and, of increasing importance, it doesn't support inter-organisational delivery – this really does need high levels of collaboration that are only possible in a teamworking environment. Finally, staying at the group level tends to foster competition within the group. A little healthy competition might not be too bad, but too much, fostered by the desire to hit individual goals, means that members of the group can feel alienated if they are struggling to deliver. In a team, the rest of the team would have a shared goal and shared outcomes so would have a vested interest in supporting a failing team member to deliver and develop. See Figure 32 below.

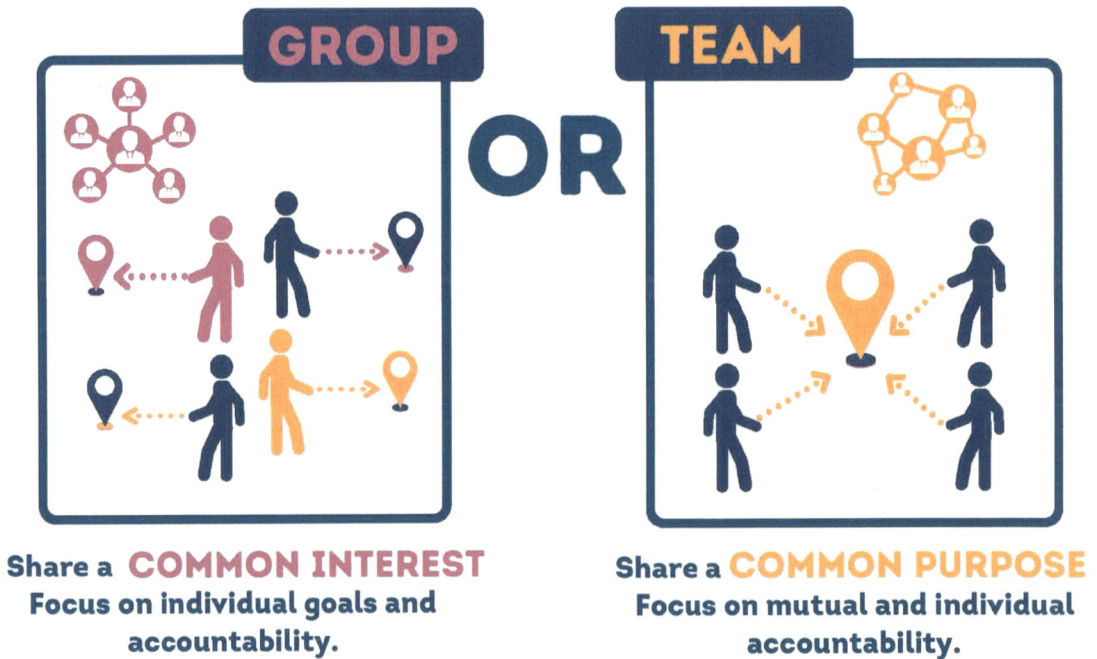

GROUP

OR

TEAM

Share a **COMMON INTEREST**
Focus on individual goals and accountability.

Share a **COMMON PURPOSE**
Focus on mutual and individual accountability.

Figure 32 - Groups and Teams: The main differences

CHAPTER 12

LEADING PURPOSEFULLY

Firstly, let's *define* what we mean when we talk about this element.

PURPOSEFULLY: Intentionally and deliberately in a way that shows determination or resolve.

Purpose: The reasons why something is done or created or why something exists; a person's sense of resolve or determination.

If you think back to the story told by Munu, the Spirit of STELLAR tells the Elders that "all creatures, including humans across all lands, needed to know what their purpose was and the role they fulfilled as individuals and together in their herds, packs, or tribes; once we knew this purpose and lived our lives to deliver it, we felt complete, we had purpose, and we were living **"PURPOSEFULLY"**". The Elders led the tribe to refocus on their purpose, and they all agreed that their purpose was:

> *To be the guardians of the country in which we live, hunt, and harvest and to protect our country so that our tribe is sustainable and our country flourishes.*

To put this into the context of a team in a real-world organisation and the individuals who make up that team, we know that, as humans, having a purpose is one of our fundamental requirements to keep us mentally well, motivated, and driven to move forward and keep going[52]. For some of us, we are lucky (or maybe we made great decisions along the way) that our personal purpose as human beings lines up with the purpose of the organisation or team we are working in.

When we feel like we belong, when there is a fit and we feel, even on the bad days, that there is a synergy between us and our work and the purpose of our organisation, it feels great. Conversely, we usually know the time is right for us to move on when we start to get restless, feel less valued, and have our personal values eroded by the way others operate in our workplace, and this is usually because our personal values and purpose don't align with either the espoused or more often "felt" values and purpose of the organisations we are

52 Clutterbuck, D. (2007). Coaching the Team at Work. Nicholas Brearley Publishing.

in. And if we can't change the organisation, then we can move to a new one.

There is a lot written about finding our personal purpose. In our coaching work, we support many leaders in organisations to do their "purpose work", and it is a life-long pursuit. But don't just have a go at it; find your purpose in your mid-twenties and then be done with it. Our booklet on Personal Purpose, which can be found on our website, www.peopleandod-partners.com, can help with this. We hope it is possible for you to see that personal purpose, organisational purpose, and team purpose are different but linked.

In Figure 33, we show that when a team's purpose is clear, all members of that team are aligned to deliver success for the organisation in which they belong[53]. Add to this a clear personal purpose for each member of that team and a clear organisational purpose and all the stars are aligned for individual, team, and organisational success.

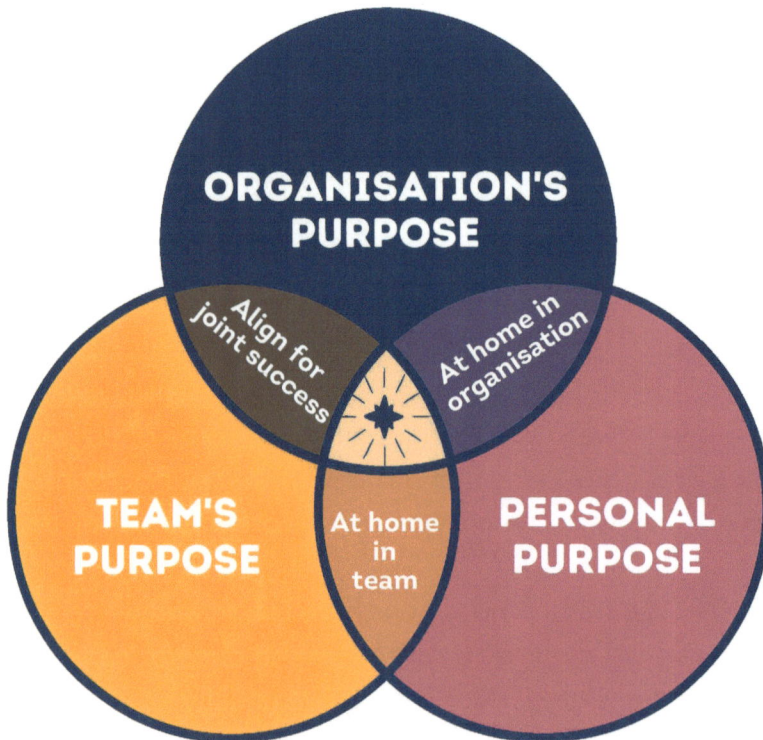

Figure 33 - Aligning Purposes: People & OD Partners Ltd 2022

---

53 Myers, G., Cliff, C., & Champoux, T. (2015). Teams that work: The six characteristics of high performing teams. Createspace Independent Publishing Platform.

Secondly – Let's *explain* what we would expect to see in the highest performing teams

The two statements we test when we ask teams to rate their maturity in this element are:

- We lead **PURPOSEFULLY** - We have a clear, shared purpose for our (leadership) team, and we describe its meaning in the same way to any colleagues and stakeholders.

- We lead **PURPOSEFULLY** - Our purpose drives our decision making and our actions, and how we deliver it displays our organisational and team values.

As you will have seen in the Maturity Matrix, we ask a team to rate whether their efforts, maturity, or success in this element are Not There Yet, a Work in Progress, or All Working Well. Based on their personal experience for the PURPOSEFULLY outcomes they are seeing in their team, they would be describing a team that is more or less like one of the statements below:

- **Not There Yet** – Can't clearly explain the purpose of this team and how it might be different to the delivery of the work of the team or the organisation. Struggles to see how the vision drives decision making and action; vision isn't clear or shared amongst the team.

- **Work in Progress** - Purpose is due for a review to determine if the team is still in alignment; clear about the direction but greater integration/cohesion needed; purpose doesn't consistently drive decision making.

- **All Working Well** - Team can clearly identify where the purpose has an effect on output, e.g., decision making implementation. Team purpose creates a passion in the team members; it is a unifying force to align differences, underpinned by team and organisational values.

We are therefore looking for evidence in a team that it has a purpose, which ignites an emotional connection to the work being done by the team, and when everything is chaotic, when sands are shifting beneath the feet of the team members and they are all pulled in different directions, this purpose is their unifying element: something they can all agree on and navigate to and from when being buffeted by the winds of change. Furthermore, delivering their agreed purpose feeds their souls, allows them to display and live their values, and enhances each member of the team as an individual.

This might sound a little flowery and may not resonate with you and your world of work. But fulfilling our purpose via the work we do, given the amount of time we spend at work, isn't too lofty a goal, surely. It is also true that if your personal purpose is about feeding your family, putting a roof over your or someone else's head, you might not be passionately ignited by the purpose of your team. This isn't what we are talking about here. This book is specifically about leaders and leadership teams. So, if you have the privilege to be a leader at any level, or you are on a leadership team, you have a duty to find your link into the purpose of that team. Otherwise, why are you taking up space in that team as a leader now?

In a real-life leadership team, doing the messy, complex business of leading, how might this present itself? What behaviours might we be seeing? There would be more of the things listed below happening than not, regularly. The team would do the following:

- Discuss whether their purpose statement was still valid and whether the organisation's context or external forces had changed to mean their purpose should change. Think about the elective clinical teams or corporate teams in hospitals during a pandemic. Countless corporate trainers and HR officers re-purposed themselves as vaccine administrators or protective equipment checkers. Countless surgical teams re-purposed some of their time as medical or intensive care relievers. They would need to know whether the purpose they had before this change was not valid for a period of time and they either needed to inculcate themselves in a new team and understand that team's purpose or, if they moved wholescale with their team, discuss the new or temporary team purpose.

- Regularly share, discuss, distribute, explain, communicate, and engage with a wider group of people in the team's purpose when it remains the same and when it changes. It is not good for the leadership team to know how their purpose has changed if everyone else who reports to them, seeks or supplies services to and from them isn't up to date or doesn't understand the changes. A purpose for a team isn't something that gets worked out at an away day then put on a poster and forgotten about; it has to be talked about or it withers and has no meaning. We probably only really know if it is out of date if, when we do talk about it, no one gets it or it doesn't ignite them with the passion required to fulfil it.

- Check others' understanding of the whole purpose and the words within it. Check that, if used, your definition of excellent, good, outstanding, etc., is the same as the next person.

- Refer back to their purpose when making decisions, when challenged with resource allocation or ethical dilemmas.

Thirdly - What happens when we *intervene* with real teams?

Whatever the data analysis shows us, it is still important for us to test our theory that purpose work in leadership teams is underdone. Therefore, one of the first things we will do when working with a team is ask them all to describe, explain, and show support for their current core purpose. In most teams, we work with their responses to the questionnaire scores an overall Work in Progress. This is usually because there is a wide range of individual scores due to the following:

- The leader usually thinks everyone knows, understands, and agrees with the purpose.

- The team often recites the organisational purpose or the operational delivery requirement of the team (for example, a team that leads the maintenance of a city's parks and gardens might say they are here to deliver beautifully designed spaces for the city that are well maintained). That isn't a leadership team's purpose; their purpose is to, for example, remove barriers, make good decisions, and secure resources so that their teams can deliver beautifully designed spaces for the city that are well maintained). We are not saying you don't need a purpose statement that describes the whole organisation's purpose, or even your part of the organisation's purpose, based on what you are there to deliver. But groups, individuals, and projects can link into those. What makes a leadership team's purpose different and what is the differentiation factor between needing to be a team or a group? Groups can work together and individually to deliver an organisational or functional purpose. Teams, especially leadership teams, need something more. For example, a recent team we have been working with has settled on a new purpose that exactly describes what we mean here; they have come up with the following:

To provide clear, credible, compassionate, and accountable leadership to everyone in XX Directorate, making it easier for all of us to do our best work for our service users and partners.

- Even if the team understands the difference between a leadership team's purpose and the purpose of the organisation or their part of the organisation, they are often not all fully aligned with the purpose statement. Some might not like certain words, some might not like it at all, some might not understand what it means to others in the group.

- New members may have joined the team and don't really understand the whole approach.

We have never carried out work with a team where this element doesn't need some attention; it is almost a pre-requisite that we cover it in some sense, as it is so fundamental to a team's success and seeing a team through inevitable difficulties along their journey. It is why it is the central element to the STELLAR MODEL® and why Munu has represented it with running water, a fundamental element to his people, to all people.

When we work with a team, our first approach will be to feedback the questionnaire, during our gallery walk, and anything that came up about the team's purpose when we carried out their one-to-one interviews. Once these have been digested and discussed, we will generally ask the team to distil or vote in some way on the issues they want to work to improve, in relation to team maturity. It has always been the case, without exception, that one of the items decided by the team for some deeper work will be purpose.

Our top five exercises for bringing about a shared agreement on a team's purpose are, in no particular order:

1. Personal Purpose Work

2. Five Whys

3. The Most Important Values

4. Team Legacy

5. Spreading the Purpose

Headlines about the exercises are given below. In our follow up book, we will be providing full directions, templates, handouts, slides, etc., about how to run the exercises yourself.

1. **Personal Purpose Work** – individually, we would get the members of the team to go through our Personal Purpose Workbook, which helps them focus on the notion of purpose and can be a great bridge to successful teamwork for them, focusing on purpose. Sometimes, people find it hard to even comprehend that this might be a necessary

piece of work they need to do, so pre-work or some time spent on this can be a great lead in. We might also use this exercise if we are working on the element of VULNERABLY.

2. **Five Whys** - in smaller groups, we get them working on answering the WHY question at least five times. The questions flow a bit like this:

a. Why does your team exist? (Possible answer: to lead and manage the delivery of X)

b. Why does your team need to lead and manage the delivery of X (So that targets get met, people get looked after, etc.)

c. Why do you need your team, now, to do that? (Because the teams need to build their own capability to do X more independently.)

d. Why do the teams need to build their own capability to do more X independently? (So that we can support the teams and build their capability.)

e. Why are you a team that needs to do that now?

The above questions and answers are just examples. If you keep the notion of five whys in your mind, this can go in several different ways. The concept comes from root cause analysis[54]. We like this process because it uses the word WHY, and this is very much at the heart of purpose work, and we will often recommend that teams read Simon Sinek's book Start with Why[55]. Also, many of our clients are familiar with carrying out root cause analyses, so the concept is familiar to them, and this helps them get stuck into it quickly. Once the smaller groups have completed their questions and answers, we might get them all to feedback to each other, or maybe mix the groups up, or keep them going to come up with their proposal for a draft core purpose statement. If we then end up with several draft statements, we will do some affinity finding work with the whole group, allowing them to come up with a single, shared, agreed purpose statement. Further work at a future session might be to focus on how they explain it to others or engage others in developing it in the future, defining what the words mean, what behaviours they describe, etc.

54 Mindtools. (2022). 5 Whys. Available at: https://www.mindtools.com/pages/article/newTMC_5W htm#:~:text=The%20method%20is%20remarkably%20simple,prevent%20the%20issue%20from%2 recurring.

55 Sinek, S. (2011). Start with why: How great leaders inspire everyone to take action. Penguin Books.

3. **Most Important Values** – we ask each team member of the team to write down (on separate post it notes) their top three or five values. (Depending on the time available, five gives you more detail to work with and three gives you enough but doesn't take so long. If you have an hour, do five; if you have half an hour, do three.) We may also need to deliver a short input session about what a value is and why it might be important to understand our most important values. We then get each team member to stand up in a line before us; they read out each value and explain how this value shows up for them in themselves and their expectations of others. Once everyone has done this for all of their values, we move along the line one by one, asking each person to hand us their post it note with their least favourite value on it. We write it up on a board, then we screw it up and throw it away in a bin. Then we repeat this until each person is left with one value each; their most important value. Writing this down, it sounds pretty brutal! It is done with love and support and has several purposes for the way it runs. Firstly, getting people to choose to throw away values gets them to viscerally connect with the value and understand its importance to them and the impact on them when someone disrespects it (in a safe and supportive place). People usually report that they really "feel" how hard it is to throw away their values. Secondly, focusing on the common ground that is shown between each other's values is sometimes a revelation and reveals more similarities than differences in the team. This can be especially useful when there are some relationship issues bubbling in the team. The further revelation for them is often when the same word, for example, honesty or integrity, can mean so many different things to people; this may then lead to other work on how they communicate clearly to each other. Finally, this exercise can be important to pull together the top values of every member of the team and distil them into the later work on the element of KINDLY, supporting a conversation on "how they show up" as leaders to deliver their purpose. When we reach agreement on those that they all share and agree on the meaning of, these can become the team values. Sometimes, we replace this with work on how the organisational values are displayed in their team. See more detail on the importance of values later on.

4. **Team Legacy** - we might ask everyone to do some personal reflection on their own personal purpose and come up with some things that might sit in their professional leader legacy statement. We might expect to see things like, "to have been known as a fair leader who developed others around them" or "to be seen as a no-nonsense deliverer of outcomes", and the variety and range can often be surprising. After some sharing of each other's content, we would then ask people to review others' legacy statements and think about the team. What would they want people to say about this team? The outcome we are seeking here is a recognition of how others may see their leadership, and the content of the legacy statements can often then be reflected in the purpose statement that they eventually settle on.

5. **Spreading the Purpose** – finally, we would usually do some work with the team on how they check on, include, and engage others in their team purpose. This is usually a session about decision making, creating a plan, assigning roles, etc.

Some *questions you might ask* yourself on this element, for either your own personal leadership style or that of the leadership team in which you sit:

- What is my purpose as a leader, right now in this organisation? What is my why?

- What is our purpose as a leadership team, right now in this organisation?

- What is our part of the organisation's purpose now? Has it changed? Have we updated it? What is our why?

- Does everyone in our leadership team know our purpose? Can we explain it? When we say it, do we all mean the same thing? Will others understand what we mean?

- Are we clear that those around us understand our purpose and understand how we are delivering that purpose? Have we sought feedback from others that this is what they want our purpose to be?

- Am I clear as a leader that I have done all I can to develop, enable, and create a clear purpose for my leadership and my team of leaders? If not, you might find the Three Top Tips a handy resource: see Figure 34 (over page).

PURPOSEFULLY
Three Top Tips

YOU

Do some work on clarifying your personal purpose; this is a life's work, and you don't have to get it right all at once and regularly review it. Get clear on your leadership purpose, what leadership legacy do you want to leave? Review your style, and write your legacy statement.

YOUR TEAM

Run a discussion with your team, find out if everyone's clear what the team's purpose is, remember it should be different to the organisational purpose or mission.
If you don't agree, or don't have one at all, do the work to create one, this might be a catalyst to begin your team's development.

YOUR ORGANISATION

Are you and your team clear about the organisational purpose?
Talk to other leaders, find out how they ensure they and their teams are structured and resourced to deliver the organisational purpose and check your own alignment with this.

Figure 34 - Purposefully: Three Top Tips

A final word on the element PURPOSEFULLY regarding the STELLAR MODEL®

There are a range of other things to look at which support a team's purpose and enable them to act PURPOSEFULLY. Having a clear purpose as a team enables a sense of belonging to that team, and this is bolstered when individual and team values are clear and can be seen to be lived, not just talked about. We will get into this some more as we unpack the remaining elements of the model. Let's take a short diversion into the topic of values to back up what we have discussed.

Values[56] – these things are our moral, ethical guard rails; they guide our decision making, they come from within, they help us do what "feels right". Brené Brown and others gave us a list to choose from[57] to help us put words to the things we feel about our limbic systems' sense of whether we are heading in the right direction – our north star. We can usually tell when we are in an "off" situation at work, in our family, or community setting as our values antennae will be twitching. Lots of us are very clear about our top three or five values, and if you ask people to name them, similar words will come up, such as truth, justice, integrity, honesty, etc. To be clear, values are traits or ways of living our life that we measure ourselves against. They are not things that we value, like our family, our children, or our way of life.

People have values, whether they know it or not, and it would be a boring world if all our value sets were the same, hence why there is disagreement and conflict. Also worth remembering is that, even if we both agree that honesty is our top value, what we both mean by that will be different. Until we have a discussion about how that value shows up in our workplace, the kinds of behaviours we would want to see, and those we would not want to see, in ourselves and others, we cannot say that we share the same values, even if the words we use are the same.

Increasingly, organisations have a set of values. Overall, this is a good thing. It means that at some level there is a code of moral and ethical conduct, a set of expectations about the way people will show up in organisations, which can be closely aligned to the behaviours that are welcomed and discouraged in an organisation. It is easy for individuals to interpret the behaviours that should be aligned against each of the three, four, or five organisational values. However,

56 Mindtools. (2022). What Are Your Values? Deciding What's Most Important in Life. Available at: https:/www.mindtools.com/pages/article/newTED_85.htm#:~:text=Deciding%20What's%20Most%20Impotant%20in%20Life&text=Your%20values%20are%20the%20things,way%20you%20want%20it%20to.

57 Brown, B. (2018). *Dare to lead: Brave work. Tough conversations*. Whole hearts. Vermilion.

that is where the overall good thing often ends.

Disappointingly, organisations often write and distribute a set of values with some descriptors, telling everyone in the organisation that these are the values we all need to live by. At one level, this seems fair enough. "This is how we are around here, and if you are not happy showing up like that, then this place probably isn't for you". That is clear, isn't it? But we don't believe that is anywhere near clear enough; let's explain more about what we mean. An organisational set of values could be something like those below, with the handy acronym of CARE, which the marketing and internal communications team will enjoy playing with.

- Customer centric
- Always learning
- Respect everyone
- Exceptional Service

If there are 20 or 20,000 people in an organisation, there will be many ways for each person to show that they are or are not living up to the organisational values by the behaviours they display on a day-to-day basis. Let's take "respect everyone" and look at that in a bit more detail. What does that mean on a day-to-day basis in an organisation? What does *respect* mean? What does *everyone* mean? Working in this organisation, should I say hello to every customer? Should I respect the privacy of a customer who looks like they want to be left alone? Should I tell my boss when I think they are wrong? Does that show respect because I am honest or does it show disrespect in this environment because it isn't the "done thing"? Or does it only matter *how* it's done? There could be hundreds and thousands of variables in this discussion as the expression of values and our understanding of what they mean is situational, contextual, and ever changing as we and the world around us changes. So, is there any point in having organisational values?

On balance, yes would be our view, but only with a few must haves that go along with them, and for us, all these things should be in place or there is little or no point in having a list of organisational values.

1. If you are going to come up with values for an organisation, don't just do it top down and roll them out; ask people what they think, do a whole system consultation, listen, and act on what you hear.

2. Once they have been agreed and decided upon, give feedback on why

they have been chosen from the wide range of input you received and why you didn't choose some that were suggested. It is only when we understand why we weren't listened to that we are happy to speak again. Put a lot of effort into communicating the values and getting everyone engaged in using them, putting them into practice.

A note of caution: there is growing dissonance sparking around the interplay between making sure an organisation or team creates psychological safety[58] and having no boundaries on what people can say and do. Let's unpack that a bit. One view is that psychological safety means setting acceptable behaviours (behaviours being the practical manifestation of living out a value or a feeling). This enables people to feel a sense of belonging; they can raise difficult issues in a safe space without fear of reprisal, or fear of anything really. An alternative view is that psychological safety means everyone should feel able to express anything they want in the way that they want, which goes against the notion that there is such a thing as appropriate and inappropriate behaviours in the workplace.

As with most things, the arguments will settle with the majority in the middle ground. The "middle ground" is when there are some boundaries in place in organisations to support our joint responsibility for the health and wellbeing of each other. One person's "acceptable" will often be another person's "unacceptable", and no matter the size of the organisation, multiply the opinions on anything by the number of people and you get difference, more difference, and so on. We fully believe that all values, core purposes, behavioural "rules", codes of conduct, etc., are great things to allow people in organisations to coalesce around, ask questions about, and make a decision towards. "Is this organisation for me?", "Does it fit with how I want to live my life, express my opinions, and show up?"

If the answers to these questions are "no, not really", then we might decide we don't belong and find a new organisation. We must caveat all of that with the view that when organisations are seeking to put purpose statements, values, behaviour codes, etc., in place, they should do it with the whole system "in the room" so that these are constructed by as many opinions as possible to provide as much diversity as possible. They should also come from a good, caring, and welcoming place, inviting challenge, free speech, involvement,

---

58 Delizonna, L. (2017). High-Performing Teams Need Psychological Safety. Here's How to Create It. Available at: https://hbr.org/2017/08/high-performing-teams-need-psychological-safety-heres-how to-create-it

creativity, risk, and the ability to celebrate failure and success. This is so that we might have a shot at creating as much psychological safety as possible, within some behavioural boundaries, allowing all types of views, opinions, and styles to feel they belong.

As humans, we want to belong[59]; some of us more than others, but all of us want to fit in to some degree in our family, in our community, and in our workplace. That sense of belonging comes from knowing the rules, written and unwritten, whether they are followed, and to what extent certain things are important. Do we use the milk in the fridge? Do we have our cameras on for Zoom? Do we use our phones in meetings? Do we talk about the boss behind their back? Do we go out for a drink after work on a Friday night? Again, as with most things, too many requirements to feel that you belong tips very easily into bullying, hazing, or initiation ceremonies. Think about the workplace for a moment and if the team bonding and "real" decisions get made over a pint after work; those who chose, for health, family, caring, or religious reasons, not to go to the pub won't be part of those decisions or feel they belong to the club that makes them. There are many other exclusions that take place every day in teams that make people feel that they don't belong, and this feeling just doesn't get the best out of us. Cast your mind back to a time when you felt excluded. Did you then go on to give your best performance? Probably not, unless it lit a fire in your belly, which might be fine for a one-time boost of productivity, but this isn't sustainable for the long term. Inclusive teams that engender a sense of belonging are the highest performing over a longer period of time[60].

59 Clutterbuck, D. (2007). Coaching the Team at Work. Nicholas Brearley Publishing.

60 Kings Fund. (2017). Caring to change. How compassionate leadership can stimulate innovation in health care. Available at: http://www.nhscompassion.org/compassion/wp-content/uploads/2016/02 Caring_to_change_Kings_Fund_May_2017-1.pdf

CHAPTER 13

LEADING STRATEGICALLY

Firstly, let's *define* what we mean when we talk about this element

STRATEGICALLY in a way that relates to what an organisation, country, movement, etc., wants to achieve and how it plans actions and uses its resources to do this.

Strategy: a detailed plan for achieving success in situations such as war, politics, business, industry, or sport; a way of doing something or dealing with something.

If you think back to the story told by Munu, the Spirit of STELLAR told the Elders that they had some vital work to do in this area to support a well-functioning tribe. Their work was to look into the future, read the signs, assess what is coming by looking up to the clouds on the horizon, and, by using their knowledge built up over many years of experience, make long-, medium-, and short-term plans that were both ambitious and achievable. This means they would spend a lot of time telling the story of what the future would be like to all members of their tribe, the various clans, and the wider group of people who they trade with and who have a stake in how this tribe operates in the future. This is called "setting the vision". They will need to be able to translate how the vision for the tribe can be achieved by explaining the main direction the tribe will take and what each clan will be doing to support this direction. We might call this "strategic planning". In a real-world team, this is about broad, higher-level themes of how the vision might be realised.

Next, they need to be able to put the large and often quite ambitious aims from the strategic plan into more practical steps, with measurements so that they know how they are getting on, such as whether they are moving towards their vision by having smaller milestones along the way. This might be called an "operational plan". Finally, and potentially most importantly, they need to be able break that down into individual tasks and outcomes for each clan, family group, and person.

To put this in the context of a team in a real-world organisation and the individuals who make up that team, we know it is very important for people in teams to know what direction they have, where they are heading. Whatever size of organisation, imagine everyone's feet pointing in lots of different directions and everyone travelling at different paces to different destinations: that would be chaotic and not much would be achieved. Now imagine everyone's feet pointing in the same direction, heading for the same destination, potentially at different paces but generally with the same sense of journey and link to a clear purpose. That is movement!

Often, especially if there is no clear purpose, there is a lack of vision or a lack of expressed and communicated vision. However, some organisations are great at this and have very clear visions, and some leaders are incredibly skilled at painting a picture of a future so clearly that people will be moved to work towards the unknown and follow that leader wherever they head. However, if this is a skill set of the leader, it might usually follow that they don't have high attention to detail and planning skills, although some very special people are great at both. What we often see in organisations is either no vision or vision but no strategy, or when the strategic plan is well written and compelling, there might not be the detailed follow through on how to make it happen and how to know when the team or the organisation have succeeded.

The vision and a passionately expressed, well narrated story about where the organisation or team is headed taps into people's emotions and their sense of belonging, their sense of purpose for being and staying in any organisation or team. There is an old and often-retold story of the time the US president asked a cleaner sweeping in a large hanger at Cape Canaveral Space Force Station what his job was. The cleaner said, "I send men to the moon". He didn't say, "I'm just a cleaner; I brush up". The name of the president changes, and who knows if the story is true, but it is a good story! What we want is for every person in an organisation to be able to see that the task they are doing at the time is contributing to the overall goal, vision, and purpose of the organisation.

To speak to the visionaries, we need to vision, and to speak to a planner, we need the plan at various levels of detail. This is what leads us into being able to lead clearly, accountably, and decisively. Something we are often called to work on in an organisation is the creation of a strategic plan, which is great, but boards and executive teams might often stop there. In which case, our challenge to them is always, "how will you know when this outcome is delivered?" The answers to the questions around how much, how many, how often, and by when often can't be answered, but you need to answer those questions to delegate jobs to others to deliver the vision. However, some teams are excellent at setting this all up and planning at great levels of detail, but they might need some support and challenge in other areas.

Secondly – Let's *explain* what we would expect to see in the highest performing teams

The two statements we test when we ask teams to test their maturity in this element are:

- Lead **STRATEGICALLY** - We have a clear vision, strategy, and set of plans for the future of our work and this team (this can be seen as the "steel thread" from idea to task output).

- Lead **STRATEGICALLY** - We spend enough time as a team "looking up and out" to plan for the longer term and understand the wider strategic drivers in our sector.

As you will have seen in the Maturity Matrix, we are asking them to rate their efforts, maturity, or success in this element by stating whether they are performing at the level of Not There Yet, Work in Progress, or All Working Well. Based on their responses, and their personal assessment from their viewpoint, for STRATEGICALLY, the outcomes they would be seeing in their team, depending on which of the three they ticked, would be:

- **Not There Yet** - Gaps in linking the vision to execution, accountability, and ownership. There is no current strategy or plan in place to guide activities.

- **Work in Progress** - The dots need to be connected between vision, strategy, and execution, working towards clarity on the vision. Effective processes need to be established to clearly link each person's role to the team and organisational goals.

- **All Working Well** - The team are clear on their strategic and operational plans; they can all see how individual effort impacts the team and organisation and vice versa.

We are looking for evidence that a team has a clear vision for the future of both their work and the team's progress and development; how the team will deliver the work with and via their sub-teams. We are then looking for a set of strategic and operational plans so that everyone can see a clear line from organisational objectives (vision, strategy, plan) to each individual's objectives (coming from their team's vision, strategy, and plan).

In a real-life team, we would want to see that, for the team as a whole, and for each individual, there is knowledge of the team's strategy and operational plans and the lines of reporting, governance, and authority are clear.

Unsurprisingly, highly mature teams would have all of this in place; unfortunately, we rarely see this being universally excellent. Many teams are good at one part of this but can't draw the steel thread from top to bottom and back again with ease. More about the steel thread later.

One of the things that teams usually fall down on is being specific enough. Proving specificity about what needs to be delivered, by whom, by when, and what success will look like when the thing is delivered. Many leaders are good at explaining the long game, the strategy, and chasing the shiny things, which is great; BUT they also need to be good at being able to describe, specifically, what it will take to deliver that long game. This includes being able to describe on a daily basis, to the people who are going to be delivering tasks and projects, etc., what 'good' looks like and what is required to complete the necessary delivery of those tasks.

Really good teams might be doing more of these things on a regular basis:

- Taking time out, probably every quarter, but at least twice a year, to look up and out and at the things that might be having an impact on their strategic direction. They might consider changing course if needed or thinking about whether the potential risks and their risk appetite has changed or needs to change.

- Checking that their vision is still valid. In response to their horizon scanning above, does that need to be modified? However, a vision should really be able to weather the buffeting winds of change for a few years.

- Holding themselves to account on the basis of the delivery of their strategic plan. Are the big themes and the programs of work required to deliver them actually happening? Do they need to move resources around or shift priorities to make them happen more quickly or in a different way?

- Clearly communicating to all the people who have to deliver the tasks what is required and finding out if the conversations happening, say at the Board, are being relayed to members of the wider organisation who are doing the tasks on a day to day basis, by middle managers.

- Analysing whether those middle managers are doing enough to explain what success will look like when delivering the strategic plan, operational plan, and tasks, so that it is easy for people to do the right thing and deliver.

Thirdly – What happens when we *intervene* with real teams?

Depending on how the individuals in a team are hard wired (and we would find that out via our data gathering and the use of psychometrics, for example), some members will be highly visionary and more strategic and others more detailed and may love the specificity of the task-based plans. In a great team, there will be a bit of both for balance to aid delivery. However, our general finding seems to be that the more senior the leaders and the broader the span of their control, the more visionary and strategic they are.

This is great and needs managing well, because a vision without a plan to implement it is just a pipe dream really. Holding a leadership team's interest on the specifics of an operational plan, if they are all easily distracted meerkats, can be hard work! This element varies a lot in how it scores across teams, depending on the make-up of the individuals and therefore the make-up of the team. Our interventions will vary based on those requirements and based on the contracting we have carried out at the beginning of our engagement, so bear that in mind; however, we do have another top five favourites here that we use time and time again.

1. **Steel Thread** – This comes from our knowledge of Human Resources (HR) and what they would refer to as the "golden thread"[61], which relates to annual performance reviews and objective setting. The premise is that if each person's objectives are set with the aim of delivering the organisational objective, then everyone is working to the same overall goals. If you are setting objectives that don't deliver the organisation objective, then either that objective is wrong or you are getting your person to do nugatory work, so something needs changing either way! We left gold behind as steel seemed stronger, more robust, and offered us a broader application away from the HR audience. We will do an exercise with teams to see whether the vision, strategy, and plans trickle down in a sensible way and then roll back up again. Do the people on the front line see their work in the overall

---

61   Marquet, L.D. (2015). Turn The Ship Around!: A True Story of Turning Followers Into Leaders. Penguin Books.

vision, etc., and the other way around? This is usually enlightening for the leadership team and often sees them simplify their vision and tighten up the way the operational plans and tasks are described. This is also a great way to get people doing "back to the floor" types of exercises or visits to outposts for hands-on experiences.

2. **Sunrise Diagrams**[62] – These are a classic strategic planning tool. We use these when the teams want to start from scratch with their vision, with the sun in the top corner of the page encasing the vision statement and each of the sun rays representing a strategic theme with the short-, medium-, and long-term projects or deliverables mapped across each theme. This is great for getting high level alignment to the themes, projects, goals, etc., but more work needs to be done later on in the detail. See our worksheet examples in Figure 35.

3. **KISS**[63] – Again, this is one that is often used to review the current plans or refresh a strategy, where we take the team through the Keep, Improve, Start, and Stop of their current plan or last year's strategy, for example. The reference will describe the categories as "Start, Stop, Continue" and you may see "KISS" in other references to project management being referred to as "Keep it Simple Stupid". We prefer our version of KISS! We simply get copies of the old documents and put up four big sheets of paper, then get smaller groups to dissect the section they are given by suggesting which parts should be listed on the Keep, Improve, Start, or Stop pieces of paper. Then the whole group might discuss how to gain agreement. Once agreement is reached, you then have the basis for a new plan for the coming year by looking up, out, and beyond the organisation to add future requirements to the existing base you have agreed on.

62 Phaal, R. (2022). Sunshine Chart Template. Available at: https://www.cambridgeroadmapping.net moretemplates#Link4

63 KISS (2022). Project Management - an overview. Available at: https://expertprogrammanagement.com/2022/02/start-stop-continue/

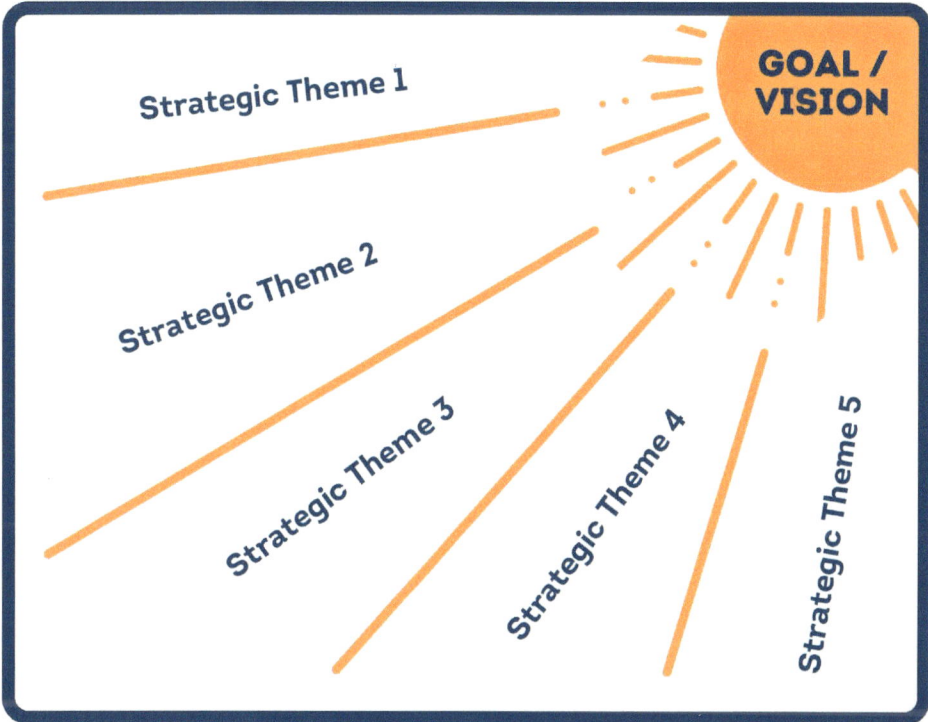

Strategic Theme 1

Strategic Theme 2

Strategic Theme 3

Strategic Theme 4

Strategic Theme 5

GOAL / VISION

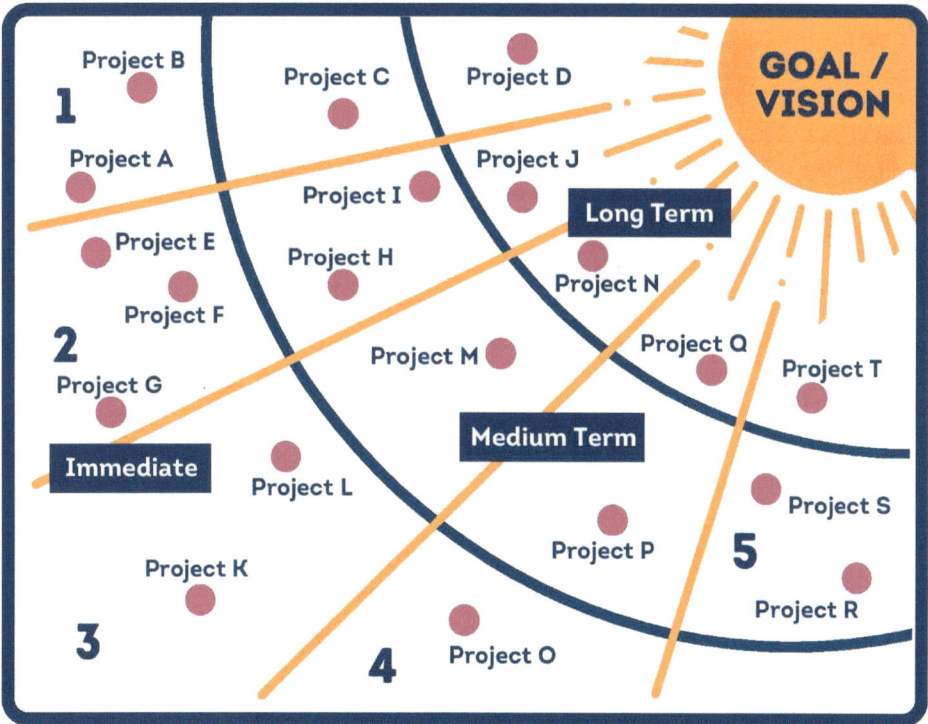

Project B

1

Project C

Project D

GOAL / VISION

Project A

Project J

Project I

Long Term

Project E

Project H

Project N

Project F

Project Q

Project T

2

Project M

Project G

Immediate

Medium Term

Project L

5

Project P

Project S

Project K

Project R

3

4

Project O

Figure 35: Sunrise Diagram Worksheet for Strategic Planning

4. **Force Field Analysis**[64] **or SWOT**[65] – either of these, or another version of this kind of outward focus, is designed to get the team looking at the pressures or expectations placed upon them by stakeholders, consumers, etc. The former specifically looks at assessing the forces for and against change and the latter specifically looks at assessing the strengths, weaknesses, opportunities, and threats facing a team or an organisation so that they can take decisions on what they might need to do to build capacity, capability, relationships, etc., in order to deliver a plan or strategy or even implement the change required. It may be that you use both of these approaches or add in some more depending on what the needs of the team are at the time you work with them.

5. **Task Roll Up**[66] - this is one of our own designs. It works really well with teams who don't think they are very strategic or who really are not very strategic in the way they think. If they are overwhelmed with enormous levels of detail about a huge volume of tasks on their to do list, it can stop them thinking strategically enough to get to the point of even having a plan, let alone a vision. If this is the case, we get them to sit on their own for a while and write down all the things that are in their head, on their various list and that they might find overwhelming: huge things and tiny things, each one on a separate Post It. This can sometimes take 45 minutes to an hour if they have a lot going on. We then get them to stick them all up on a wall, and we have seen whole rooms covered in Post Its from this exercise! Once everyone has had a cup of tea, we get them to go around and read them all, and as you might expect, there is a lot of repeat tasks, issues, and comments. We get everyone engaged in a big theming exercise, moving around the Post Its until those that describe similar tasks or seemingly immovable issues are all together, and they are then grouped again so that the ones that relate to similar themes are together. Usually, in our experience, there is generally around five to eight overarching themes. These might be along

64 Swanson, D.J. & Creed, A.S. (2014). Sharpening the Focus of Force Field Analysis, Journal of Change Management. 14(1), 28-47, DOI: 10.1080/14697017.2013.788052

65 Jacobs, T., Shepherd, J., & Johnson, G. (1998). Strengths, weaknesses, opportunities and threats (SWOT) analysis. In V. Ambrosini, Exploring Techniques of Analysis and Evaluation in Strategic Management. (p.122). London: Prentice Hall.

66 Exercise from the resources section of People & OD Partners Ltd contact admin@peopleandodpartners.com

the lines of workforce, technology, budget and resources, safety and quality, research and education, operational delivery, and targets. The next step is to get smaller teams in the group to own a theme or two and distil the Post Its into admin tasks and issues so that what we end up with is five to eight strategic themes, rolled up from the huge lists of tasks, and a manageable amount when distilled again and again. Each team reports back and pitches the theme and the tasks to the whole room, and we work from there. It is strategic planning from the bottom up, but when a team is stuck in the weeds, it is a great way to pull them up to the blue-sky thinking.

Some **questions you might ask** yourself on this element for either your own personal leadership style or that of the leadership team in which you sit:

- Do you have a current vision, strategic plan, operational plan, etc., that you understand, that the team understands, that is a working document you can measure your success with on a regular basis?

- If you talked to someone on the front line of your business delivery, would they see a link between what they do and the organisational vision, strategy, and plan? Do they see themselves as part of a bigger picture?

- Do you think it is important in your organisation that your people do see themselves has having a role in delivering the bigger picture?

- Are people's objectives, on which their performance (potentially with a knock-on effect to their pay) is measured, directly linked to the organisational vision, strategy, and operational plans?

- When was the last time you took part in a strategic planning session or took time out to think about the future of your team, your part of the organisation, the risks and issues that were on the horizon?

- Would you describe your team as "down in the weeds" or more "up in the clouds"? We use these two metaphors to describe overly detailed thinking and overly strategic thinking, respectively.

STRATEGICALLY
Three Top Tips

YOU

Assess your own preferences for the strategic or the task, the transformation or transactional and work out where you may need some development, then either develop deeper skills or build your team around you to complement each others' skills. The best teams have a mix of both.

Build in regular strategic planning sessions with your team, where you look up, and out and really take stock of what is happening in the world around you in relation to the world inside your team, and check for alignment, dissonance, and whether your plans are still relevant.

YOUR TEAM

YOUR ORGANISATION

Can you see the "Steel Thread" running from the organisational vision, to front line delivery teams? If not, take some time to draw a line on a board or piece of paper and plot the various editions of the story that is currently told, then begin to fill the gaps in your organisation's "Steel Thread".

Figure 36: Strategically: Three Top Tips

CHAPTER 14

LEADING DECISIVELY

Firstly, let's *define* what we mean when we talk about this element.

DECISIVELY: quickly, effectively, and confidently, in a way that strongly affects how a situation will progress or end.

Decision: a choice that you make about something after thinking about several possibilities.

If you remember what our Spirit of STELLAR said about this in Munu's story, making decisions (rather than not), implementing those decisions, and communicating them well across the whole tribe was vital to their success. The Elders were the ones making lots of the big decisions for the tribe. They needed to make sure they had enough information to make the right decisions and that they were able to explain why they had made them, what they were, and, most importantly, what everyone had to do to enact the decision.

Let's consider the role of a board of any large organisation. Essentially, the fundamental role of a board is to make decisions. They make these based on the information provided to them. Once assured that the information is correct, that they have considered wider issues, and that they have enough information, they decide. Then they expect the managers in an organisation to act upon their decision and deliver an outcome. Following that, they seek assurance that past decisions have been implemented and that all tasks are on track to deliver the outcomes required to keep the organisation running well and in steady state, anticipating emerging risks and seeking to grow and/or change considering the anticipated future operating conditions.

The management of any organisation needs to make decisions all the time to keep the operational flow of an organisation going, be they big, small, complex, or easy decisions. It is fair to say that most leaders will cite making decisions as one of the key roles of their job.

But how effectively is this done? What do we expect to see in places that are acting decisively and are good at decision making and all it entails? Don't make the mistake of thinking that this element is only about the single acts of deciding between one course of action or another.

It is about the big and small decisions, how they are made, how they are enacted, how they are communicated, and how the leaders assure themselves that they have been delivered and that people are acting differently as a result of the new decision.

Secondly – Let's *explain* what we would expect to see in the highest performing teams

The two statements we test when we ask teams to test their maturity in this element are:

- We lead **DECISIVELY** - Once we make a decision, we support, purposefully implement, and communicate that team decision (especially when it wasn't our personal preferred choice).

- We lead **DECISIVELY** - We are always clear about the specific actions needed to implement our decisions (who is doing what, when, how, and what's next).

What you will see from the Maturity Matrix is that, depending on their answers to the questions, we would see the narrative describing the way the team has scored, as follows:

- **Not There Yet** - Decisions are not made at all or as a whole team. There is a lack of clarity around which actions need to be taken and communication of decisions is poor or inconsistent.

- **Work in Progress** - Reaching decisions can take some work with various opinions and perspectives competing for agreement. Decisions can sometimes be affected by outside influences. The gaps or overlaps between teams are unclear, which makes specific actions tricky to allocate with clarity.

- **All Working Well** - The team operates with empowered decision making and with high levels of mutual supportiveness. Everyone is kept informed and is clear on the steps to take and who is taking them.

In a real team, how might this show up? There would be more of these things happening than not, regularly. The team would be:

- Going through items in meetings and making decisions based on the available information. These would be recorded and communicated, along with the actions required of people to implement them.

- Avoiding making decisions in corridors or outside meetings, because this is when they miss the opportunity to have all voices inputting information to enable the widest possible participation in decisions. Of course, in reality, leaders make decisions on day-to-day issues all of the time; not everything needs to wait for a meeting, although it is important to have an agreed set of topics on which a team absolutely need a team approach to decision making. Working out as a team which decisions need to be discussed in a meeting is a task in itself.

- Seeking the verbal agreement, sign up, or support of every person in the room regarding the decision as it is made and clarifying that everyone knew what it meant and what needed to happen next, along with allocating actions for people to take responsibility for.

- Agreeing a communication plan for announcing the decision outside the room and enacting it across the organisation.

Thirdly – What happens when we *intervene* with real teams?

What we see time and time again in leadership teams that we work with is that it either takes them an eternity to make decisions, which might be endlessly deferred to get more data or information, or they don't really take many decisions at all, but they think they do.

Let's unpick those two statements. Depending on our basic make up, we either make gut instinct decisions, using our sense, feelings, and experiences (then find the data to fit the decision we have already made), or we keep hunting for the right decision in the data.

As leaders, we need to be able to notice our preferences (for example we might have a preference for lots of data before we reach a decision). We must also be able to act counter to our preference. Sometimes, we might be called upon to make a quick, instinctive decision, and we have to work hard to get comfortable with that. This also works the other way around. When we prefer to trust our gut, there are times when we must study the data first. However, a note of caution: sometimes, the calls for more data are a handy way of putting off making tough decisions because enacting the decision will be hard.

Taking too long making a decision may also be due to having other "stuff" lurking behind it. It may be that the differing opinions are too hard to work through or that the issue itself is really complicated. However, we have to remember that, as leaders, leadership teams, boards, and other senior groups, it is what we are paid for! If there is no other purpose to our team, it is to make decisions, so we might as well get as good as we can at it.

The final point to make on this element, before we get into our top five exercises for a team, is that we hear "we really need to make a decision on that" after a long discussion and then there is no clear decision made or recorded, just lots of agreement that a decision is needed. Hence our creation of the DISCO model, see Figure 37 (what a great name!), which pulls together all the elements required to make a good decision, the most fundamental being to actually make one.

Five of our favourite exercises to support the element of DECISIVELY are:

1. **DISCO of decision making** – This covers all the elements required, firstly ensuring that the team specifically **defines** the decision they are trying to make and that everyone in the team defines it in the same way. This is often the first stumbling block in making effective decisions. Secondly, the team gathers as much relevant and appropriate **information** as they need to make the decision now. Thirdly, the team has a really good discussion and consideration of as many possible **solutions** to the issues they are trying to decide on as possible. This requires excellent attention to lots of the other elements of the STELLAR MODEL® for a really open team culture. Fourthly, the team **chooses** and implements the best solution for their situation. It might not be the most popular decision, but it should be the best for the situation and the organisation (notably not always best for individuals or even members of the team making it). The word "implement" is quite important here too. One of the biggest issues for teams is making sure that everyone in the room is in agreement, or at least can support the decision outside the room, and that each person knows who is going away to do what to implement the decision. Further, it is important that it is well communicated across the parts of the organisation or wider than it needs to be. Finally, and an often-forgotten part of the process, have some sort of review process built in so that the team can review whether the decision they made and the **outcomes** it created were the right ones. They might even go further and review what brought about the issues that meant they had a decision to make in the first place. Could that have been avoided? We would usually use some form of live decision required by the team to work through all the stages of this as a learning opportunity for

THE DISCO DECISION MAKING MODEL

Where is your team strong and where could you get better?

DEFINE

INFORMATION

SOLUTIONS

CHOOSE

OUTCOME

Most teams are good at some parts of this. Often, verbalising that we are "all in" and making sure we have the right information is harder.

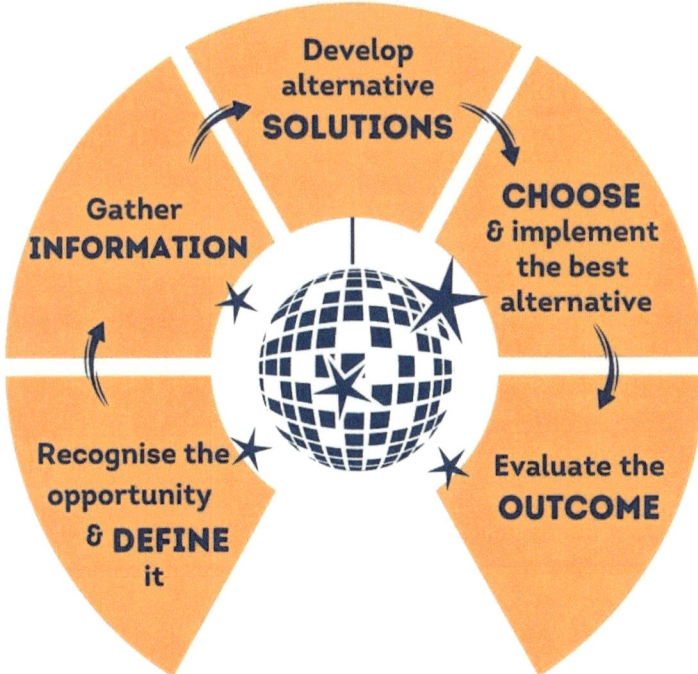

Develop alternative **SOLUTIONS**

Gather **INFORMATION**

CHOOSE & implement the best alternative

Recognise the opportunity & **DEFINE** it

Evaluate the **OUTCOME**

Figure 37: The DISCO model for decision making. People & OD Partners 2018

the team, maybe getting thems to assess where they are now on each element and where they need to be for the future.

2. **All At Sea Exercise** – You don't have to use this specific exercise but depending on the level of experience in making complex decisions, we might run a scenario of some sort. All At Sea is the exercise where you imagined you are stranded in a boat with a set of weird and wonderful items but can only use three of them to get you to safety. Which ones would you use and why? Facilitated well, made into a team competition of sorts, it works really well to get everyone to listen to options or opinions, and there is a huge array of scenarios out there, or you can make up your own. Better yet, use a method that could be specific to the sector you are working in.

3. **Cartesian Co-ordinates**[67] – Put simply, this is a mathematical approach for pinpointing distances from two fixed points, which can be multidimensional. For our purpose, we are using them to view decision outcomes. This comes from our coaching work, where we often get coachees to answer questions, especially when they say they don't know the answer or don't know what to do. Essentially, the Cartesian Questions are:

- What will happen if I do this?
- What will happen if I don't do this?
- What won't happen if I do this?
- What won't happen if I don't do this?

These sound almost the same if you skim the questions, but they are powerfully different and distinct, and they are really worth getting teams familiar with so they can view an issue through a few different lenses.

4. **Covert Processes** – This is some input from us on the work we have referenced before, largely by Bob Marshak. We would take the team through some work to look at the subconscious thoughts they may be having, versus the words expressed, where this comes from, and how it impacts the team. We would link this to work in the KINDLY element. The reason why we often place it with work on this element is that it

67 Wikipedia (2022). Cartesian coordinate system. Available at: https://en.wikipedia.org/wiki/Cartesian_coordinate_system#:~:text=A%20Cartesian%20coordinate%20system%20(UK,the%20same%20unit%20of%20length.

is often the things behind the scenes, the political, relational issues that cause decisions to become complex and which are often behind the lack of decision making. What might not be said in the room is "we can't do that because it will upset X or Y" or "they wouldn't like it". It means that the wrong decisions are often made to cover up covert processes, especially people-based decisions, and our work in this element is to do the hard graft on what is "under the table" so that it is easier to make the right decisions.

5. **Decision Deployment** – This is all about making sure the work done on decisions in the leadership team room doesn't stop there. How does this get communicated? How does the team make it easy for them to seek assurance that what they have decided is now being implemented? Are there report back loops? Is it easy to see? Is it automated? Or are they just crossing their fingers and hoping it will all be all right once they decide? We will usually map the decision implementation, communicate and action loops using some form of process mapping or other testing of the feedback loops. We will probably do this with a real live issue and might support the team with testing their views that this area is working well, by some mystery shopping or other consumer-related experience testing.

Some *questions you might ask* yourself on this element for either your own personal leadership style or that of the leadership team in which you sit:

- Am I a gut instinct or data-hungry decision-maker?

- Whatever my preference, can I do the other one too or do I need more development?

- How does my team go about making decisions? Are they made in the room or in the corridor before we come in?

- Do we put off hard decisions?

- Are decisions implemented and communicated well in my organisation?

- Can we be sure that, once implemented, decisions "stick"? Are we assured that everyone is enacting our decided approach at all times across the whole organisation?

DECISIVELY
Three Top Tips

YOU

Reflect on your approach (using all the elements of the DICSO model), your preferences, and the impact that your ability in this area has on your colleagues and teams. Could this be an area of personal development for you?

Employ some of the approaches we use in our exercises with your team, e.g., perform "rounding" at the end of a discussion and ask for a decision from each person or ask them to replay the decision they think you have all reached. You might be surprised at the responses!

YOUR TEAM

Can you take some time to check across the whole organisation whether people know about and are delivering decisions your team has taken? Phone a few people up in other departments, or better still, walk about and see for yourself.

YOUR ORGANISATION

Figure 38: Decisively: Three Top Tips

CHAPTER 15

LEADING ACCOUNTABLY

Firstly, let's _define_ what we mean when we talk about this element.

ACCOUNTABLY: to act as though you own the totality of what you are responsible for and are able to give a satisfactory reason for it.

Accountable: responsible for what you do and able to give a satisfactory reason for it.

Think back to the story told by Munu. This element is about everyone in the tribe knowing their personal role in getting things done, in delivering the direction that was set by the Elders. It is also about every person in the tribe, once they understood what they had to do, showing a level of commitment and accountability to get it done, saying what they were going to do and doing what they said they would: being reliable.

One of things we come across time after time, especially but not solely in the public sector, is a lack of being able to comfortably hold people to account.

When we lead others and when we are in a team with other leaders, we all have tasks to complete for those we lead and for the wider health of the group. One of the main ways people trust us to be part of their group or to lead them is that we do what we say we will do, or to put it another way, we deliver on the tasks we have either explicitly agreed to or implicitly agreed to do because they are in our job description. When we fail to do these, people have three choices: they can either call us on it, "Hey, when are you going to do that thing?", they can ignore it because it doesn't matter too much to them or the organisation (in which case, why was it one of our tasks? – back to clarity of role), or they can not mention it but fester on it so that it becomes an unspoken issue, either unspoken in its entirety or unspoken to the offending person, but potentially spoken to others in or out of the team. In which case, this becomes an issue that the team has to face.

Holding ourselves to account, doing what we say we will do, is vital for team trust and team delivery. Beginning to be able to hold each other to account around the team while not making it a personal attack on the individual is a skill. (Does the person need some development?) Is this skill lacking or is it the will that is lacking? (In which case, does the person need to be on the end of a bold conversation?)

The example we set as leaders is vital to being able to roll out performance management or what we have sometimes called "Accountability Meetings" across an organisation. For example, if we brought different sections of an organisation together each month to show support for their efforts and celebrate their successes and hold them to account for their key performance indicators and targets, this would only work if the leadership team were known for doing what they said they were going to do and being accountable themselves. This approach, which we have used in many settings, creates a culture of accountability if the meetings are well run, rather than a culture of personal attacks on the individuals. It genuinely creates a place where the leaders are seeking to understand what they can do to unblock what is stopping delivery. This is an area that usually requires quite a bit of work in most teams!

Secondly – Let's *explain* what we would expect to see in the highest performing teams

The two statements we test when we ask teams to test their maturity in this element are:

- We lead **ACCOUNTABLY** - We are clear about our own deliverables and KPIs and understand everyone else's in the team

- We lead **ACCOUNTABLY** - We hold each other to account for delivering what has been agreed and we discuss and commit to new approaches to support each other's delivery.

What you will see from the Maturity Matrix is that, depending on their answers to the questions, we would see the narrative describing the way the team has scored as follows:

- **Not There Yet** - Lack of clarity around performance indicators; unsure what the KPIs of others are; limited discussion around performance beyond immediate and short-term deliverables; people not held to account. If an attempt to hold team members to account is made, it is taken personally.

- **Work in Progress** - KPIs need to be reviewed to ensure they are still fit for purpose; imbalance of knowledge of KPIs and deliverables; methods for holding one another to account could be improved/clarified.

- **All Working Well** - The team are clear about what their individual KPIs and deliverables are and how they interact with others' KPIs; this knowledge means everyone can be held to account appropriately, with support and challenge. This isn't taken personally.

In a real team, how might leading accountably show up? There would be more of these things happening regularly. The team would be:

- Talking openly about their targets and performance, what has been achieved, and what they need help with from others; challenging others if they are being held up from delivery because another member of the team has not done what they said they would.

- Clearing action points in minutes before they get back in the meeting room and not signing up to a delivery date for something they know is unrealistic, then not meeting it.

- Clear, consistent, challenging, and supportive of each other's teams in regular performance accountability sessions so that there is a collective and shared ownership of overall targets.

- Linking the tasks that are being delivered with the overall strategic and purpose-led delivery for the whole organisation.

Thirdly – What happens when we *intervene* with real teams?

One of the first things we would do with teams is work out with them their level of understanding about the difference between accountability and responsibility and how they view that in their team. The issue is that these words are often used interchangeably when, actually, they mean quite different things. For us, the simplest explanation is you can delegate responsibility for a task to get done to someone else, but you can't delegate the fact that you are accountable for it being done. You are **accountable to** someone else (we all have a boss), and you might also be **responsible for** getting a whole range of things done. It is a bit more complicated than that, and Eagles Flight[68] have a great resource if you want to read about it some more.

As with the other elements, we have a range of favourite exercises we use with teams, in no particular order usually, but we would often do number one first.

68 Eagles Flight (2022). Want your people to embrace the future? Mindset is Everything. Available at: https://www.eaglesflight.com/asia/

1. **Accountability Ladder** - We want to get the team to understand their own and each other's approach to personal accountability. One of the tools we use the most with clients is Stewart's Accountability Ladder[69.] shown in Figure 39. Essentially, what Stewart is saying is that our response to events, or how we show up in order to complete tasks, sees us displaying either victim behaviours or accountable behaviours. The victim behaviours see us responding to situations by saying things like: "Well, I didn't know I was supposed to do that"; "no one told me"; " if only she had done what she was supposed to, I wouldn't be in this situation"; "I can't do it now, it is almost the end of my shift"; "I sent them the email, so I have done my bit, so if I do nothing else, then maybe it will all go away". This is a set of responses about the world doing things to us and us being in a passive, things-happen-to-us state of mind.

Alternatively, the accountable behaviour responses are all about us acknowledging reality, for example, counting the chocolate bar wrappers in our car and telling ourselves the reality that, as we have been the only ones driving around in it all day, we must have eaten the five chocolate bars. Of course, in a work setting, this could be akin to the four reports that we were supposed to submit by the end of the week that still haven't been written because we haven't either delegated them or committed enough time to them.

After a bit of self-talk, we are then able to own our part in the issue at hand, make a plan, or come up with a solution, such as not taking anything chocolate-based into the car or planning better for the report writing deadline. Then we put in place the support or resources that we need to make the first step happen, then the next and the next.

Like most of the tools we use, this isn't a miracle cure, making you be self-accountable overnight. Our purpose when using these tools with clients is to bring it to their attention, so the next time they find themselves saying or thinking, "Well, it isn't my fault", they might just think, "Oh dear, I am showing up in the bottom half of the accountability ladder. What am I going to do to move myself up the rungs?" Or better still, they will use one of our other tips, which is to give some

69 Stewart, J. (1984). The Role of Information in Public Accountability. In: A. Hopwood and C. Tomkins, Issues in Public Sector Accounting. (p. 13). Oxford: Philip Allan Publishers Limited.

Accountable Behaviours
Things happen because of you

Make it happen
Find solutions
Own it
Acknowledge reality

Wait and hope
Excuses (I can't)
Blame others
I don't know

Victim Behaviours
Things happen to you

Figure 39: The Accountability Ladder, Stewart 1984

trusted people around them the permission to give them feedback, and someone else might say to them, "Hey, I just wanted to say that you seem to be showing up on a bottom rung. Is that what you want? Is that what you intend?"

2. **Delegating Effectively** - In order to be able to hold other people to account, we need to have things in place: we need to have clarity on who is supposed to be doing what, role clarity, and we need to delegate effectively, especially if we are the leader.

Role clarity is covered in more detail in Chapter 16 on the element CLEARLY, but let's talk about delegation for a bit. This regularly seems to be tricky for a lot of people, potentially due to how hard we seem to find it to communicate clearly, provide feedback kindly and clearly, and have what we might consider to be difficult conversations.

We run through our model for effective delegation and get the team to put this into practice outside the session and come back with some feedback about how it went using some different approaches for:

- What – specifically what are you delegating?
- Who – have you chosen and for what reason have you chosen that person?
- When – have you set deadlines, check ins, report backs?

- Authority – do they know the bounds of their delegated decision making?

- Follow Ups – how are they keeping you updated? Have you got the three questions that will assure you they are on track?

- Feedback – are you regularly giving them feedback on the task and on how they are approaching it, citing what went well and what could be even better?

  As you might imagine, delegating effectively is almost always a place to pause with a leadership team as some people are more comfortable with this approach than others, and a leader's approach to this can be a cause of tension in a team.

3. **"My Expectations"** – We use the creation of this with leaders in our coaching work and when we are working with a team. Several of us have used this process when leading teams ourselves, and it is quite a simple way of setting the expectations of your team and allowing them to challenge you when you don't live up to your promises. It holds you to account as a leader. The process is that you write up no more than two pages about how you work, what you need from the team, when you need to be informed, involved, consulted, etc., and what kind of behaviours you might expect from them, and them from you, then you send it out to all your team members. We have seen these done really well and not so well. The key is that they should be short, specific, and humble, not preachy. Let us know if you want some great examples to copy for your team and be prepared for someone to hold you to account on it, so be careful what you sign up for in your My Expectations document!

4. **Forward Plan & Follow Up** – One of the things that breeds a lack of accountability across your teams and organisation is if the most senior leaders set a bad example. We are often surprised when we talk with leaders and their teams about the leadership operating model, their cadence for meetings, and team engagement. For example, it is often the case that team one-to-one meetings get cancelled, leaders' team members come to catch ups with not much preparation, and agenda items are often not completed between meetings. This is understandable a lot of the time, but there is no excuse for the lack of accountability that poor practise in this area breeds. What we want to see is a regular team cadence of huddles and check ins, operation and

strategic meetings, and one-to-ones and that they all have a pattern, which means everyone knows that they need to be prepared for them, step up during them, and follow up after them. We have lots of tools and templates to set the teams up well to roll this out across their organisation. This approach alone can be a powerful force in setting an accountability culture across a whole organisation.

5. **RACI/V/S/** – This is a project management tool at its heart but works really well with all leadership teams when they are trying to delineate who is responsible, accountable, and so on, for what in their team. The RACI terms stands for:

- **Responsible** is the one doing the job
- **Accountable** is the one who owns the outcome of the job, that is, he is the go-to person if the task is not getting done. Generally, they have the authority to replace the responsible with another person if the responsible is struggling
- **Consulted** is asked non-binding opinions and advice on how to do the job
- **Informed** is updated with the progress unidirectionally and has no input on the task

In process terms, we would get the team to pull together a quick table, popping the tasks along one side, and heading up some columns with the letters R, A, C, and I along the top. After a discussion they should agree which single name should sit in the table at the intersection of the task and the column for responsible, accountable, consulted and informed.

You can add to this to suit your operations with other letters, for example, V, S, O, S, T, and D.

- **Verification** is the role for someone who checks the results
- **Sign-Off** is the role for the person who has authority to decide if something goes ahead, stops, or pauses
- **Out of the loop** describes someone who might need to be considered who hasn't been so far?
- **Support** is the role for those who might provide some form of support
- **Task focused** describes those who are working on specific tasks
- **Decides** highlights the roles of those who are decision makers

A word of warning: keep it simple. Too many letters make it more complex than not having an acronym at all, and RACI works pretty well and is a good place to start.

Some **_questions you might ask_** yourself on this element, for either your own personal leadership style or that of the leadership team in which you sit, include :

- Do you display accountable behaviours? Do you follow up and hold yourself and others to account?

- Could you develop your skills in that area so that when you hold people to account, you do it with skill, so it isn't personal but is about the work and the behaviour, not the person?

- Is it clear in your team who is supposed to do what, when, and how? Does everyone share the knowledge of where they are up to and the dependencies on others to deliver?

- What is the wider organisational culture like in regard to account-ability? Are people held to account? Do people do what they say they are going to do?

- Do agenda items regularly go undelivered and get carried over to new meetings without challenge?

- Can you assess people's behaviours against the accountability ladder? Are there more victim or accountable behaviours on display?

ACCOUNTABLY
Three Top Tips

YOU

If you sometimes find yourself responding by displaying victim behaviours, and we all do by the way, either give someone permission to give you that feedback or notice it yourself and try to stand back acknowledge the reality you are in and make a plan, then take the first step.

YOUR TEAM

Have a discussion with your team about the difference between accountability and responsibility. Carry out a RACI on the causes of friction, the things that never seem to get fully resolved. The conversation alone will bring about some improvements.

YOUR ORGANISATION

Is there an accountability culture and is there forward planning and follow-ups? Can you introduce a better or different or just consistent cadence of meetings, preparation, and follow-ups from them so everyone is expected and expecting that tasks that have been agreed *will* be done?

Figure 40: Accountably: Three Top Tips

CHAPTER 16

LEADING CLEARLY

Firstly, let's *define* what we mean when we talk about this element.

CLEARLY: Without doubt; obviously; in a clear manner with clarity

Clarity: The quality of being certain or definite

If you think back the story told by Munu, the Spirit of STELLAR told the Elders that they must make sure everyone was very clear on the role they played in their clan and tribe. Everyone needed clear expectations about what they were supposed to do each day to keep the tribe running well, and importantly, they needed others to understand, be clear, on who was doing what, where each person's role began and ended. It would be no good for everyone to be off hunting with no one gathering wood. It was also important for everyone to know how to tell each other whether they thought they were living up to the roles they had agreed to take on; to be able to give (and receive) clear feedback. This way, everyone could improve how they were doing, learn to work together even better to get things done, and support each other to learn skills that the whole tribe needed. Finally, the Spirit of STELLAR told the Elders that they as leaders needed to be really clear when they were passing on information so that every member of the tribe got the same message, in enough time, and with enough simplicity so they could take the right action required of them. They needed to communicate clearly.

This element is new in the STELLAR MODEL®, but it is something that we have noticed has been lacking in leadership for a long time, we just hadn't quite found the right words or the right place for it in our model. Before adding it as a specific element to the STELLAR MODEL®, it still came up in our work with teams. Usually, it surfaced, linked to accountably, decisively, and several of the other elements. The regularity with which we were covering the need to be clear, to have clarity in several areas, led us to create the extra element earlier this year.

Why is this so important that it needs its own element, you might ask? It is probably due to our beautiful languages and vast diversity of experiences leading our meaning, understanding, and expectations, when unsaid or not stated clearly enough, being translated differently. To explain this a bit more, even what we think is the clearest possible instructions for a task, "please take the report upstairs" (you can pick anything you want), could be open to misinterpretation.

There is no mention of timing, urgency, which report, which level upstairs, to whom it should be given, or whether it should be left on the stairs, and we could go on and on.

When we leave things open to interpretation, they are just that: interpreted by others in a way that makes sense to them. There is room for confusion, things to be misunderstood, and this pertains to all we do as leaders, so being clear on a whole range of things is really important when seeking to get things done in organisations.

Secondly – Let's *explain* what we would expect to see in the highest performing teams

The statements we test when we ask teams to test their maturity in this element are (remember this element was new in 2022):

- We lead **CLEARLY** - We clearly and regularly discuss with our wider teams our expectations of their roles and what and how they will and will not deliver.

- We lead **CLEARLY** - We are comfortable with and skilled at giving and receiving clear feedback from/to each other in this team.

As you will have seen in the Maturity Matrix, we are asking them to rate whether their efforts, maturity, or success in this element falls into one of the categories below:

- **Not There Yet** - Feedback is not given in a timely or respectful manner, and when given, it is taken personally. There is little clarity about role boundaries and who or which team is responsible for what. Low levels of team and wider communication and engagement.

- **Work in Progress** - Comfortability with feedback and how it is given or received varies within the group. There could be more clarity about roles and more communication to wider team members and within the team.

- **All Working Well** - There are competent skills and a positive mindset around giving and receiving feedback. There is clarity about roles and who is responsible for what, and there is clear communication and engagement within the team and beyond.

Therefore, when a real leadership team with the usual pressures they are placed under are operating well around this element, we would expect that they are able to:

- Provide role clarity both verbally and in any written documents, reinforcing what people are asked to do, e.g., job descriptions, recruitment advertisements etc, so there is a clear understanding of role breadth and boundaries.

- Give clear feedback and have the skill and will to do so. See Figure 41 for an explanation of what we mean by this.

- As well a ensuring the skill and will of feedback is high, make sure that "bold conversations" happen, things don't get left to fester, this links to many of the other elements, but is important to restate here.

- Work on all levels of communication. Being able to communicate well, simply, clearly, and especially in an upfront way, is vital to trust and a feeling of safety and belonging. There are often difficult messages to convey and as leaders and leadership teams communicating clearly, without a lot of corporate speak or waffle is what everyone wants. Often, we treat our wider organisational teams more like children and try to protect them, when they are more likely to trust and respect us if we treat them like adults and communicate clearly and with kindness and compassion.

Thirdly – What happens when we intervene with real teams?

In our experience of working with a team, this simple element is often not explicitly talked about. However, once we ask a few questions about how people feel giving feedback, having bold or difficult conversations, or how clear the roles are, there is usually a realisation that their world of work could be a lot clearer. Therefore, we run a series of exercises with the team to explore how they can gain more clarity, and the following five exercises are some of our favourites.

1. **Giving & receiving feedback** - We get the team to practice on each other while we and others provide feedback on them providing feedback (this can get a bit complicated if you are not careful!), using the process in Figure 41.

THE SKILL

| People know how to deliver feedback effectively | People know how to receive feedback effectively so to encourage more feedback |

THE WILL

| People want to deliver feedback to their colleagues | People genuinely want to receive feedback from their colleagues, and not just the good stuff |

GIVING FEEDBACK — **RECEIVING FEEDBACK**

WHEN ... HAPPENS
specifically describe the behaviour

LISTEN ACTIVELY
don't be planning what you are going to say, just listen

I FEEL ...
specifically describe your reaction

ASSUME GOOD INTENT
you will get more from the feedback if you assume it is given with love

BECAUSE .....
explain why you feel this way

AVOID BECOMING DEFENSIVE
if you have to speak, just ask clarification questions

WHAT I IMAGINE IS ...
if possible, show you understand what's behind the behaviour

PROVIDING FEEDBACK IS BRAVE
give them time to talk; understand they might find it hard

WHAT I'D PREFER IS ...
suggest a different way of behaving

BE THANKFUL
feedback is a gift to help you improve

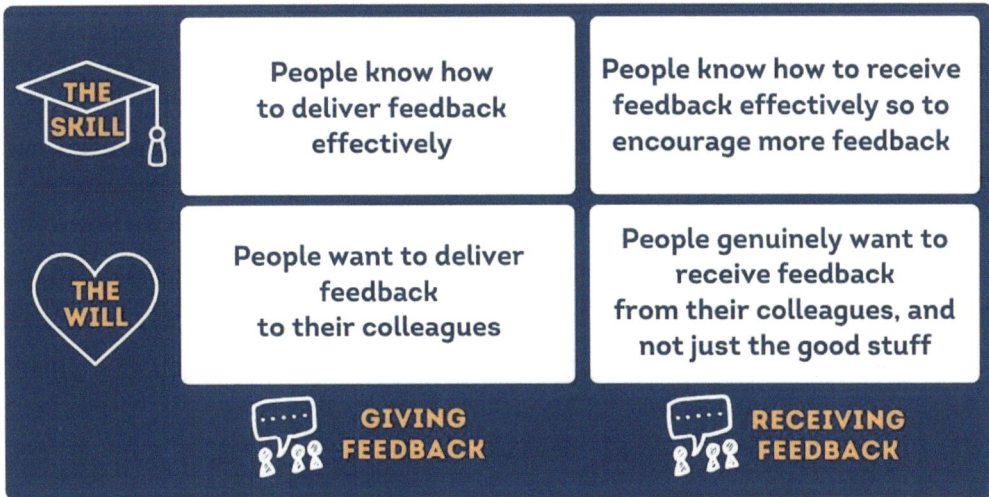

Figure 41: Giving and Receiving Feedback Process, adapted from NVC Rosenberg[70]

---

70 https://www.nonviolentcommunication.com/learn-nonviolent-communication/4-part-nvc/
Puddle Dancer Press 2019 Michael B Rosenberg

2. **Bold Conversations** – We share with the team our process and methodology for having bold conversations. (These conversations, though bold, should not always be considered negative or challenge-based conversations. Some people struggle to have praising and celebratory conversations too!) This requires them to do work before, during, and after the conversation and be clear on the purpose of the conversation, the commitment to the change they are seeking, and the follow up that will take place. This can be quite a big topic, and we run whole seminars on this alone as it is one of the things that is avoided by leaders and managers the most in organisations. The Brené Brown quote of "clear is kind" applies here too as so many people pad out the discussion with lots of fillers when clarity and kind directness is what is most needed.

3. **Role Definition** – Everyone needs to be clear on their role, and this links to lots of the other elements, but it is always a worthwhile exercise to go through with the team, having them explain their roles, their team's deliverables to each other. It might sound simple, but a team should be able to understand the parts of the team and the whole team make up and explain that to new starters, for example. You might be surprised by how many leadership teams don't really know what each other actually does. A step on from just explaining to each other is to get them to rate each other's delivery, gives tips for improvement, and tell them what they do really well. This also supports giving and receiving feedback!

4. **Rewriting JDs/RDs** – In a similar vein to the exercises above, we will often ask leaders to strip back their job descriptions to be crystal clear, and we will ask them to modify them to add not just what they need delivered, but how they need it delivered. Working in this simplification for their direct reports, or even for their own job description, always seems to remove layers of complexity, and adding behaviours or ways of working also enables you to hold people to account much more easily for their mindset and approach, as well as the delivery of more challenging outcome targets.

5. **Communicating Well** - Four Words – In order to support all of the work we do with leaders and their teams, we generally need to do work on communication in some form or another. One of our favourite exercises is the Four Words. We get people to individually come up with a definition of four random words. Often, we will use quite emotive words, such as love, money, justice, or freedom, and ask people, once they have got their definition of them, to join with another person and come up with an agreed joint definition. Then the two people join another two people, and so on, until we get an agreed definition for the four words across the group. This is a great exercise in so many ways, but it really brings home for the team how important clarity of communication is when you are saying something.

Some *questions you might ask* yourself on this element, for either your own personal leadership style or that of the leadership team in which you sit, include:

- Are you clear of your role and what people expect of you?

- Is it apparent that everyone else in your team is clear on those things too?

- Do the written documents back up what everyone thinks their role is, and if not have you reviewed role descriptors, job advertisements, and recruitment advertisements lately with a critical eye? Are they clear, simple, SMART? Could anyone, anywhere understand what they mean?

- How does feedback work in your team? Are you good at giving feedback and receiving it? Could you be better?

- What is your team like at an organisational level regarding clarity and feedback? Are communications clear? Could you do more to be clearer in how you and your team communicate, perhaps setting an example?

- Can you review your recent communications and or get an objective person to do it, are they clear, simple, easy to understand, or could they be better?

CLEARLY
Three Top Tips

YOU

Take a bit of time to review your approach to giving and receiving feedback. Work through the process we use, see if you take all the steps, and brush up on the areas where you could improve.

YOUR TEAM

Can you and your team look at how you communicate with those who report to you? Could it be simple and more clear? It would be worth reviewing some meeting minutes or decisions that have been communicated and asking a range of people what they think the meaning is.

YOUR ORGANISATION

Could you review the job descriptions, recruitment advertisements, and other similar documents relating to your areas of work and make them clearer, more simple, and easier to use? Get clear with people about what is expected of them, and give clear feedback.

Figure 42: Clearly: Three Top Tips

CHAPTER 17

LEADING KINDLY

Firstly, let's *define* what we mean when we talk about this element.

KINDLY: in a kind way; (of a person) having a character that is generous, helpful, and caring about other people

Kind: generous, helpful, and thinking about other people's feelings:

Think back to the story told by Munu. The Spirit of STELLAR tells the Elders that having agreed standards of behaviour, what is and isn't acceptable, is important. It is an agreed way of being together and an agreed way of challenging each other, when the behaviours fall short of what has been agreed, that begins to get everyone used to striving to meet the standard that has been set.

Sometimes, when we work with teams, especially when we first raise the concept of having a behaviour charter, when writing down what is and isn't felt to be acceptable in the team, there is push back. This might be about the fact that someone in the team will feel they don't need it: "We all behave well most of the time". Or they might say, "We all get on well already". We have even had some team members say that they felt it was childish and like being at school when they have to sign up to how they are going to behave.

In the face of those responses, we would a) move on to other work or work on another part of the model for now and b) notice who in the team isn't saying anything about the behaviour or c) look out for unspoken but contrary reactions to those who are against the work. These may be the people who would really like an overt agreement but might not yet feel able to come out and say it.

What has always happened is that, as we move through the rest of the work, unacceptable behaviours will surface. While in our head we might be saying to ourselves, "I did think we should have talked about a behaviour contract", what we might do is ask whether the team would like to consider revisiting drawing up a set of behaviours and discussing what is and isn't acceptable.

As part of our group process facilitation or team coaching role, we would be noticing the behaviour, the culture, the "feel" of the team and taking the right opportunities to ask questions about their behaviour to each other, to ask about team norms, and to hold up a mirror to the team for them to decide if their behaviours need any work. They usually do! There are things to work on to tweak even the most caring and compassionate teams.

Secondly - Let's *explain* what we would expect to see in the highest performing teams

The statements we test when we ask teams to test their maturity in this element are:

- We lead **KINDLY** - We show care for each other in this team; we know each other well enough to know when extra compassion is needed.

- We lead **KINDLY** - We have an agreed code of behaviour in our team and feel comfortable apologising when we lapse.

As you will have seen in the Maturity Matrix, we are asking them to rate whether their efforts, maturity, or success in this element falls into one of the categories below:

- **Not There Yet** - A formal behaviour "code" has not been established; unacceptable behaviours are not challenged; there are low levels of psychological safety. There are some factions/cliques within the team.

- **Work in Progress** - Code of behaviour needs reviewing to ensure new team members are included; relationships still need to be cultivated amongst the team. There is some psychological safety.

- **All Working Well** - There is an authentic desire within the team to support and help each other grow as leaders and individuals; codes of behaviour are established and adhered to; people easily speak up and apologise.

In a real team, in real life, when doing the messy, complex business of leading, how might this show up? There would be more of these things happening than not, regularly. The team would:

- Be checking in with each other regularly and really wanting to know the answer to the question, "How are you?"

- Be open with each other enough to get to know the team's various needs and triggers and be able to tell when something isn't quite right.

- Be able to challenge each other when behaviours are not up to standard, take it well, not personally, and apologise to each other for any transgressions.

- Be able to move beyond empathy with each other towards compassion and show self-compassion so that they can set clear boundaries to look after themselves and each other.

- Be able to translate that into the behaviour they show to their teams across the organisation, in the decisions they make that impact people, and in the way they work on a daily basis.

Thirdly – What happens when we *intervene* with real teams?

Again, we have our top five exercises with which we work when covering this element in teams, and in no particular order, we have highlighted them below.

1. **Behaviour Charter** – We've mentioned this quite a bit already, and it is a key exercise we run again and again. In our experience, it isn't enough to get a list of behaviours, as they will mean different things to most of the people in the room. One person's "supportive" will be another person's "suffocating". We get all the team members to come up with specific behaviours that they think show that someone is behaving in a supportive way, for example:

- Asking me if I am ok

- Saying good morning

- Making me a coffee

- Offering to check my report draft

   Then they come up with specific examples of when people are definitely not showing that they are supportive, otherwise known as contraindicators of the behaviour, for example:

- Ignoring me in the morning

- Not responding to emails regularly

- Not offering to help

- Asking me if I am ok, but then not listening to the answer

   The remaining part of the exercise is explaining to each other our interpretations of the display of behaviour and agreeing on a few phrases and examples that we can all use to explain to others what the behaviour means. These then usually form part of the printed charter.

2. **Iceberg** – This is a classic, but we return to it time and again to explain the basics to our attendees. It might seem simple to show a picture of an iceberg, which depicts the bit above the water as the behaviour (because that is the bit you can see) and the layers below as deeper or more hidden thoughts, feelings, beliefs, perceptions and values (which can't easily be seen). However, it often forms lightbulb moments for the team when they understand that the parts they are seeing in themselves and others on the outside are the external manifestations of thoughts, feelings, beliefs, perceptions, and values and, at the very core, are usually some form of unmet need. When we start to talk about our unmet needs, or even just the concept of behaviours being a manifestation of unmet needs, it can be a revelation for teams; it brings out a level of compassion for each other that wasn't present before.

3. **Compassionate Leadership** – Following on from that, we are able to then do some work with the team on how they might bring about more self-compassion to their approach and then be able to provide compassionate leadership. Again, this often requires some explanation about the fundamentals of self-compassion or self-care, resilience, and mental toughness, for example, and how being a good role model in this for our teams is itself a good thing, but also about how to move from sympathy to empathy to compassion.

4. **Coffee Conversations** – This is a really simple and effective process to put in place for teams so they can get to know each other. See our handout in Figure 43. Getting to know one other better as people develops tolerance, more understanding, and more compassion. It also engenders trust.

5. **When I am...** – This is a version of needs and wants. We ask all members of the team to think about them when they are at their most stressed or pressured and when they are most liable to display unhelpful behaviours around the team. We then ask them to consider what they need from their teammates. Do they need to be left alone? If so, for how long? Do they need a hug, a coffee, a cake, or to be left alone for a while then asked if they need any help? This allows them to reflect on how others experience them and practise stating their needs to others. Their statement might look something like,

COFFEE CONVERSATIONS

INNER MIDDLE OUTER

THE PURPOSE

To connect on a personal level with your teammate,
to practise listening with kindness, and to understand
what drives your teammate. You find out a lot about yourself,
especially when saying some of it out loud!

THE PROCESS

Make a coffee catch-up 1:1 date with your teammate and take
turns going through a series of topics, providing information about
the level of depth you feel comfortable in: inner, middle, outer
(meaning, deepest, some depth, surface level, respectively).
Label the level of depth you are choosing and tell
your teammate about

PAST   - your childhood, upbringing, education
PRESENT   - your family, friends, hobbies
FUTURE HOPES - you dreams and aspirations
FUTURE FEARS - what holds you back

This isn't a work 1:1 - don't talk shop, talk people & relationships.

Figure 43: Coffee Conversations Handout

"When I am up against a tight deadline and a bit stressed out, I grow quiet and more introspective, and, at first, I need time on my own, and it will stress me more if people come to ask if I am OK, so I will close my door and would prefer to be left alone. After a few hours, I then need someone to come and see if I am OK and maybe bring me a doughnut!"

For this leader, his team asked him to pop a red sheet on the outside of his door when he didn't want to be disturbed and take it off again when he wanted some support.

Some **questions you might ask** yourself on this element for either your own personal leadership style or that of the leadership team in which you sit include:

- Do you care about the wellbeing and happiness of the people in your team? Can you see that other people in the team care too?

- Do you feel cared for, looked out for, by members of the team?

- What is it you might need from them and they from you to feel cared for?

- Do you defend your team members if you hear others speaking in a negative way about them?

- How do you feel about working with your team to come up with a behaviour code or charter, one that is written down and you all physically sign up to?

- How would you encourage people to challenge your behaviour if they find it unacceptable or even if it makes them feel slightly uncomfortable? What signals are you giving off that show you are ready to hear feedback and not just compliments?

KINDLY
Three Top Tips

YOU

Are you kind to yourself? Do you show yourself enough compassion? Pause and reflect on your own self-care and self-support, and the level of challenge you place on yourself. Make some time to look after yourself regularly - you can't pour from an empty cup!

YOUR TEAM

Have you got a written down behaviour code or charter for your team?
If not, create one. The work to get to an outcome will bring about debate and might bring up some examples of the behaviours you want to jointly challenge!

YOUR ORGANISATION

Your organisation might have a set of values? Does everyone know what they mean? Which behaviours show they are being lived or being trodden all over?
Ask around,
find out whether other teams have done this work, and learn from their experience

Figure 44: Kindly: Three Top Tips

CHAPTER 18

LEADING CURIOUSLY

Firstly, let's *define* what we mean when we talk about this element.

CURIOUSLY: showing that you are interested in learning about people or things around you

Curious: interested in learning about people or things around you:

If you think back to the story told by Munu, "curiously" meant for the tribe that they needed to be tolerant, respectful, and look beyond behaviour that might anger or frustrate them. If they could summon up curious thoughts and wonder about their own reactions to others' behaviour and where the behaviour of others came from, what caused it, they might be more accepting of different approaches and different ways of doing things.

Embracing difference was vital for the survival of the tribe. They needed lots of different types of people to ensure they had the resources to tackle lots of different issues that came before them. Having all the same skills or all the same ideas wouldn't help them too much when issues came up that they had not faced before.

The Spirit of STELLAR also alerted the Elders to notice that what is going on across the whole tribe, who is included, who takes the lead, who is excluded, and that what isn't said is sometimes more important to notice than what is said. Bringing things out into the open and talking about them in a measured way, when they are "small" things, might feel like it takes time, but it is a lot better in the long run than ignoring things until they become a "big" issue.

This element is all about two things really. It is about capitalising on what Deepak Chopra[71] calls "The Gap". That is, the gap between action and reaction, pausing to wonder, to be curious about our reactions to others' perceived transgressions and taking time before we respond in what might be an unhelpful way. In the same vein, it is about turning that curiosity inward and reflecting on our hard wiring. What or who pushes our hot buttons and why is that? Does it still serve us well? If not, can we let it go, move on?

71 Chopra, D. (2014). The Gap. Available at: https://www.deepakchopra.com/articles/the-gap/

This element is also about our favourite phrase when working with teams: "notice and name". That phrase pretty much sums up the role of a group process facilitator. When performed with skill, this causes a group to pause and think about whether their behaviours, reactions, and actions are still fit for purpose and serving their team well. When we work with teams, we are huge advocates of throwing out the whole rug, never mind just making sure that there is nothing lurking underneath it. Of course, this must be done gently and with care, holding the team in a place of safety while the work is being done.

Secondly - Let's *explain* what we would expect to see in the highest performing teams

The statements we test when we ask teams to test their maturity in this element are:

- We lead **CURIOUSLY** - We are comfortable discussing and resolving conflict and other uncomfortable issues, such as "groupthink" or perceived power in our team. We don't leave issues "under the rug".

- We lead **CURIOUSLY** - We stay open and curious about our reactions to what other people say and do and their reactions to us, without being judgemental.

As you will have seen in the Maturity Matrix, we are asking them to rate whether their efforts, maturity, or success in this element falls into one of the categories below:

- **Not There Yet** - Perceptions of power make it difficult for others to speak up and challenge; sayings like, "It's just how we do things around here" are frequently used and stifle discussions around challenging the status quo or challenging those in power positions. Diversity of thought and experience is not welcome and often "shut down".

- **Work in Progress** - Some things should be brought to light earlier; some things are left undiscussed to minimise conflict; there are times when some might not feel comfortable speaking up; some things need to be handled with greater tact.

- **All Working Well** - The team welcomes diversity of thought, experience, and approach, knowing that this brings more creative solutions. The team feels comfortable to "call out" situations early and has the skills to discuss constructively and reach future-focused conclusions.

In a real team, in real life, doing the messy, complex business of leading, how might this show up? There would be more of these things happening than not, regularly. The team would:

- Raise issues as soon as there was a hint of tension. You know that icky feeling you get in the pit of your stomach that tells you something is wrong? Well, that is the time to raise it. Raise it gently with a question; something like, "I'm sensing we are all having a bit of trouble with this issue. Do others agree? Should we all say what we think and then have a discussion about it?" If things are left, they will grow, get a bit more gnarly, and then, if we are not careful, erupt into a huge issue that sometimes needs external help to heal.

- Be open to being challenged on their views and opinions, on decisions, on anything really. We show that we are open to challenge by our reactions. Wondering where the other person is coming from and asking genuine questions is a much better reaction than defensiveness.

- Be able to embrace conflict. See it as a positive difference, which, if well managed, surfaced, and talked through, can get a much better outcome.

- Always seek to understand ourselves. Most importantly of all, the job of any leader is to constantly be working on themselves as leaders, to always be open to development and feedback on where they need to develop.

One of the things that often upsets the dynamics in a team is either a lack of curiosity or, as will be discussed more in the next chapter, an inability to appear vulnerable by being curious. What do we mean here when we say that leaders must approach leading curiously? A leader and a leadership team have a duty to look past what is presented as the primary issue across a number of settings, many of which are covered by the other elements of the model. While it is right to be curious about decisions, role clarity, and accountability, etc., we won't cover that here because that is covered in the chapters relating to those elements.

For this model, a leader behaving curiously would be asking questions about people's behaviour, working out what covert processes are going on between members of the team.

Thirdly – What happens when we *intervene* with real teams?

This is one of the most interesting elements as it picks up the area where most people can get a bit uncomfortable and can cause conflict in teams. Lots of people prefer an easy life in the short term and don't want to deal with issues where they might feel uncomfortable and have to deal with other people's feelings and emotions, especially when lots of people can't deal with or express their feelings and emotions.

However, it is essential in the contemporary world of work that we are able to bring our whole self to work, even our feelings and emotions, positive and negative, and our role when working with leadership teams is to support them to make it easier for them to have difficult discussions, to disagree and still have a great relationship.

We have our top exercises in this element too, and in no particular order, we will use some or all of the following:

1. **Conflict Styles** – These might come to light for each member of the team if we have carry out individual and team psychometric tests, or if not, we have a simple questionnaire that we use during a session for the team to assess their own conflict style. We would then use the results to base a discussion around the needs of the group and individuals when conflict arises.

2. **Mediation** – More often than you might think, when we get asked to work with a group, there is real conflict and tension, sometimes outright hostility between two or more members of the team. This might mean that we can't work with the whole team until we mediate between those where the tension is present. It is really hard and probably serves no purpose for the wider team to try to begin team coaching when there is very evident hostility between a few of the group. If they are not willing to participate in mediation, we will decline the assignment. The leader of the team must take some responsibility for setting the acceptable and unacceptable behaviours in their team, offering a solution, and then holding people to account if they fail to seek the support offered.

3. **Choice Impact Model** – this is a great model developed by our fabulous long-time collaborator, Diane Wilkinson, of Connecting to Excellence, and is shown in Figure 45. We use a range of exercises around this model to surface the difference between intent and

impact in relationships and how we can choose to take the view that "the other person's responses are their issue and I can't do anything about it" or that, if we want a different impact, we have to have a different intention.

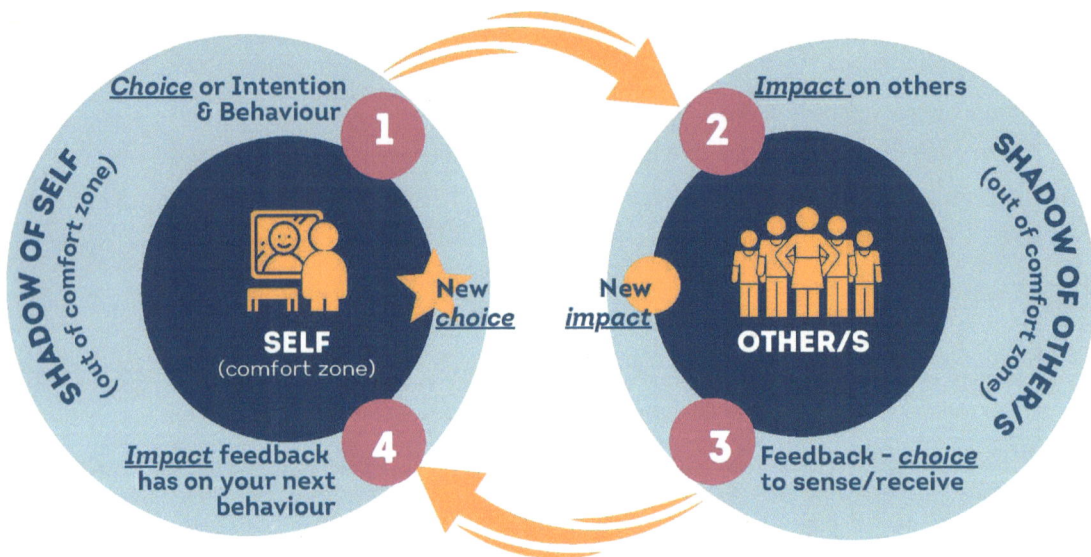

Figure 45: Choice Impact Model – Diane Wilkinson of Connecting to Excellence

4. **Transcending orange** – this one is popular time and again, and some teams we worked with years ago still have their dried-up orange on their desks. You will need some oranges for this exercise. We like to give everyone an orange to keep at the end to remind them of the exercise! The basics of this are that you use two stuffed toys or two of the team and they have one orange, which they have to work out how to share, without just splitting it in half! This might seem a logical option, but both only get half an orange then! What other options can you think of that provide more of a win/win, where both people come out with a whole orange, or more? You can run quite an in-depth exercise as people come up with ideas, which can then be themed into a variety of outcomes with each side seeing themselves either in a win/lose, lose/win, lose/lose, or win/win outcome. Our aim is to get the teams to come up with outcomes that transcend the conflict altogether. You can come up with some ideas yourself and work out which category the outcomes might go into! For example, planting the seeds could mean oranges for everyone, forever (eventually).

5. **It's not you, it's me** – this is a great exercise to do with people in pairs. As the facilitator, you come up with a range of innocuous statements, such as, "When will you have that report ready by?" and "What is the delay with the project about?" In each pair, one person will innocently deliver the statement and the other will, on purpose, uncharitably re-interpret it in the way they might if they're searching for negative subtext. They phrase it starting with, "I heard", as in, "You asked when I will have the report ready, and I heard 'You're working too slow, speed up.'"

The first speaker refutes this with an "I meant" statement. As in, "You heard, 'you're working too slow', but I meant, 'I need to know a timeline so I can plan the rest of my day.'" This chain can end after discovering the underlying meaning and can proceed to the discussion of the disconnect between what one party means and what another hears. This activity can reveal for the participants that subtext may have a very different meaning, even if it seems clear, because each person lives in their own context. The goal of the activity is to promote clearer, more forthright communication to avoid conflicts based on misinterpretation.

Some ***questions you might ask*** yourself on this element for either your own personal leadership style or that of the leadership team in which you sit are:

- What is it that really winds me up about the behaviour of the people in my team or others at work in general?

- I wonder why that is or where it comes from?

- What is it that I might do or say, a way that I behave, that might have the same impact on others?

- What is the atmosphere like in my team? Are people open, supportive? Do they listen? When do tensions arise and what are they?

- How do we deal with those tensions as a team? Do we avoid them, discuss them, or take them out of the room?

- How comfortable do we seem to be as a team when discussing difficult issues or disagreeing on a decision or approach and having a really robust discussion until we reach a unified way forward?

CURIOUSLY
Three Top Tips

YOU

One of the most important things we must do as leaders is continue to focus on our own personal development. Be curious about your own reactions to others' behaviour. Wonder what it is that hooks into you or pushes your hot buttons; can you let any of that go?

Notice what isn't said in your team meetings and what things might be "under the table" and might need a discussion. Use some gentle questions to ask, "others in the team have noticed that we opt to take a lot of things outside the meeting" for example.

YOUR TEAM

Does your organisation have "speak up safely" policies, informal dispute resolution processes, and does the culture feel like one where it is safe to raise issues that need talking about? If not, can you find out whether some of this could be introduced across your organisation?

YOUR ORGANISATION

Figure 46: Curiously: Three Top Tips

CHAPTER 19

LEADING VULNERABLY

Firstly, let's *define* what we mean when we talk about this element.

VULNERABLY: behaving in a way that allows you to be easily physically or mentally hurt, influenced, or attacked

Vulnerable: able to be easily physically or mentally hurt, influenced, or attacked

The basic dictionary definition does make it sound like we are asking you to be really exposed as leaders, and in a way, we are. Not so you can be physically or mentally hurt, but so that people feel that they can (with the bounds of decency and respect, being kind, clear, etc.) say what they feel they need to, expose their weaknesses, and state their needs and wants. Others will only do this if they trust us, and they will only trust us if they can make a connection with us on a personal level of some sort. To make that personal connection, we need to expose our own vulnerability.

If you remember the story told by Munu, this was about the Elders being prepared to say that they didn't always have all the answers; that they sometimes needed help. Acting in this way helped the tribe trust them and feel able to speak up about what needed changing or ask for help themselves. It also gave a clear signal across the tribe that owning up to mistakes and seeking help to do better is a strong and brave thing to do, not a weakness.

Gone are the days of the hero leader who tries to save the day to show they are invincible and can do everything themselves. However, the macho style, command, and control leadership is a skill that is still required sometimes in certain emergency scenarios or when responding with speed at times of great change. This means that leaders sometimes need to able to flex their skills to utilise that approach. Much of the time, they will get better results from their teams if they show a level of vulnerability and have the courage to trust their teams with some of their worries, ask for help, and occasionally declare that they don't know what to do, but encourage the team to work together to find a way forward.

Secondly – Let's *explain* what we would expect to see in the highest performing teams

The two statements we test when we ask teams to test their maturity in this element are:

- We lead **VULNERABLY** - There are high levels of trust in this team; we are credible in our roles, reliable and authentic, consistent, and have integrity.

- We lead **VULNERABLY** - In this team, we are comfortable admitting mistakes or asking for help as we value the delivery of team goals above individual achievements.

As you will have seen in the Maturity Matrix, we are asking them to rate whether their efforts, maturity, or success in this element fall into one of the categories below:

- **Not there Yet** - Low level of trust and respect throughout the team; individuals value individuality/self-promotion over team results, functions are siloed and mistakes or difficulties hidden.

- **Work in Progress** - Good acknowledgement of interdependencies but not enough time to appreciate and celebrate achievements; trust levels still being cultivated; some team members are trusted more than others; some team members are not considered "team players". Errors are reported but blame shifting might still occur.

- **All Working Well** - High levels of mutual respect and trust throughout the team; the delivery of team or organisational goals is placed above individual achievements. People easily ask for help or hold up their hands to admit errors and ask for support.

Therefore, what we are really looking for in any team is how much they say and don't say to each other, how much they open up, and what is left unsaid. When we observe teams, this often tells us much more than what is said.

This is about trust, which is a difficult area to work on with teams. If only you could run a workshop on trust and then trust would magically arrive in the team and all would be well. However, it isn't as easy as that. Each and every element of the work we do with teams builds trust, if done well, even when the topics are difficult to talk about. One of the things we will use with teams to really simplify the concept of trust in their work is the Trust Equation from The Trusted Adviser by Charles Green. It goes a bit like this: $T = R + C + I \div SI$. Trust (T) is gained by being:

- Reliable or knowing your stuff (R)

- Credible or doing what you promise to do (C)

- Intimate or, in this context, allowing people to know enough about you to connect with you and feel safe with you (I)

That trust is divided or worn away by evidence of your self-orientation or self-interest/self-importance (SI/SO). (You can substitute this with any other word that provides evidence to people that you are only in this for yourself!)

In a real-life leadership team, how might this show up? There would be more of these things happening than not, regularly. The team would:

- Share when they need help, ask for support, and admit when they had got things wrong or didn't know the answer.

- Be open about how they felt, what their resilience was like, or whether they were struggling more generally.

- Be able to bring their whole self to work, their experiences, background, views, hopes, and fears, and support each other's aspirations and worries.

- Be genuinely interested in what makes the other members of the team tick and seek to understand those around them.

Thirdly – What happens when we *intervene* with real teams?

Some teams have high levels of trust overall, and in some, there are one or two closed personalities, or newer people, whose levels of trust and ability to show vulnerability might need some work. This isn't just up to them; it is up the whole team to show that they can be trusted.

The top five exercises we often return to again and again, because they work so well, are the following (in no particular order):

- **Turning Points** – This comes from the work of Bob Dick[72] who has a really straightforward PDF online with the process outlined, and I have been using this for a number of years, either in team coaching or in large scale interventions to connect people. We also ran a series of Turning Points sessions for our FLAG webinars in 2021, which gave birth to the Inspiring Women ∞ Inspiring Women series of books. Needless to say, we are big fans! It is quite a simple, yet very powerful process, which consists of

---

72 Dick, B. (2018).'Turning Points' activity. Available at: http://www.aral.com.au/pdfs/02turningpoints.pdf

reflecting on the key people, events, places, etc., that mark turning points in your life and sharing them with others or a partner in a small group. This sharing allows reflection and a consideration of whether the things that caused the situation to be a turning point are still helpful to you as a leader or whether some things can be let go. Each smaller group might then share some or all of the content with the wider group, perhaps what they learned and what surprised them about the others' turning points. You can expand, contract, or modify this to suit your attendees, although remember the power of what can often be quite deep reflections and revelations from the group.

2. **Shields or Cut Outs** – This exercise can be used as a connection exercise and is just a bit different to (and potentially a bit lighter to) the six boxes exercise below. The Shield is just what it says: we create a template of a shield with a banner along the bottom for the attendee to list their motto, and it would usually have four quadrants to the shield. These can be titled in any way you choose, but we most often go with something along the lines of:

a. Most closely held value

b. Lifetime ambition/bucket list item

c. Thing you would save if your home was on fire (other than people!)

d. Personal pride/ regret

For the Cut Outs, these are usually cut out shapes of people, and we get attendees to use our craft box and decorate them to depict a shirt that gives a statement about the person, a facial expression that shows how they are feeling, plus some footwear that shows where they are heading in life, and so on. You can go a bit wild with these two, as long as you bear in mind what your aim is. That is to get people to open up about themselves and share information to build the "intimacy" element of the trust equation.

3. **Six Boxes** – This is a build on the exercise above and has the capacity to be used in more depth, taking a bit longer and with a smaller team. Plus, it allows you to build other elements in. The six boxes are drawn on a piece of flip chart and contain pictures which show:

a. How you would like to think others see you

b. Your most closely held value

c. Something from the last year that you personally regret

d. Something from the last year that you are personally proud of

e. The way you see this team now

f. The way you want to see this team in the future

You would then get each of the pictures up on the wall, asking the artists to describe their drawings to each other. Some care does need to be taken with this exercise. People should be encouraged to be as open as they can, but also reassured that the depth they go into is their choice. The personal regret might be having one too many biscuits with their cup of tea that morning. It is what it is, and that alone is data for you to work with as you support the team. However, our experience is that this exercise, when well facilitated, is a gold mine of data and pays huge dividends for the team. Without exception, teams have discovered things they didn't know, shared emotional revelations, and found new ways to support each other. This exercise is very much a favourite!

4. **Appreciate & Frustrate** – This exercise is one we often use, but only if we have been working with a team for some time and they want or need a deeper level of connect. We link this to the CLEARLY element in the STELLAR MODEL® and provide this to support the ongoing development of giving and receiving feedback skills in a team. The process is to make sure the team understands how to give great feedback and has some of the skill and will to do this in a kind and supportive way and then ask them to collate what they appreciate about the way each of their colleagues behave and what frustrates them about the way each of their colleagues behave. We provide them with a sheet to note them all down, and then we deliver this feedback in several ways depending on the maturity of the team.

What works best is meeting in a 1:1 with each person, giving them the feedback we have received about them: appreciate and frustrate. They will then review it, acknowledge it, and, in a future session, tell their colleagues that they have listened, heard, and committed to carrying on doing what is appreciated and asking for help to work on what is frustrating.

5. **Check In & Out** – We support all the teams we work with to incorporate this exercise into their meeting formats; most importantly, the Universal Check In. This is all about humanising the workplace, making sure that team members can connect their head and heart, i.e., the things that go on in the workplace and our personal feelings about it. It is quite an easy process and means that all the team meetings start the agenda with running through their highlights and lowlights since the last time they met. They should try to give a work example of both, and it is of great importance for them to explain how that example made them feel. For example:

"My highlight in the last week is that we finally got approved the business case we have been working on for months, and it makes me feel so *happy and proud* of all the work my team and I personally have put in.

My lowlight for the week has been the high level of follow-ups I have had to do with a couple of members of my team to get them to provide responses on the risk register. It made **me feel despondent and as though they don't understand the importance of it as a process** and that I must be doing something wrong in how I am explaining it."

Everyone in the team takes a turn, then the chair sums up the sentiments in the room and pulls out any themes that might need to be put on another meeting's agenda, and it is the responsibility of team members to check in on anyone who shared deeply or seems like they might need a bit of extra support outside the meeting.

I can't tell you how powerful this has been for the teams we have worked with. This one thing alone changes the nature of relationships in teams for good. See our worksheet for running the Universal Check In (Figure 47).

UNIVERSAL CHECK IN

HUMANISING THE TEAM RELATIONSHIP
There is no right or wrong way to do a check in!

THE PURPOSE

1. Helping the team to relate to each other as a "whole" person.
2. Affirming the balance of interplay between head and heart.
3. Getting to know each other better.
4. Sharing our "heights", as well as our "depths".
5. Finding opportunities to support each other.

THE PROCESS

A. Share the high/lowlights at work since the last meeting.

HIGHLIGHTS- Something that was exciting, was positive, I was proud of (for myself and others), got me all geared up and recharged my passion for work, made me feel supported, etc.

LOWLIGHTS- Something that discouraged me, felt like "I was not going anywhere in spite of," problems with people, being misunderstood etc. Opportunity for support and ideas.

B. At the end of the check in, someone (can be anyone apart from the chairperson) should summarise the state of the group before moving on to the main business of the meeting:

> Sounds like we have a lot of positive things to celebrate...

> A lot has happened in the last couple of weeks: some good and some bad. Anything we need to take further?

C. It is important that during lunchtime, tea break, or even after the meeting, team members take time to acknowledge what an individual has shared during the check-in, especially if they risked being vulnerable by sharing how they felt.

Figure 47: The Universal Check In Handout

The Check Out is a bit different, but is used for similar reasons, and, unlike the Check In, can have a few modifications depending on the team. Essentially, its purpose is to reflect on how the team worked during a meeting or session they were holding. The questions they might ask can range from:

- What Went Well (WWW) and what could have been Even Better If (EBI) – this is a favourite to get teams started on this concept
- Do we think we lived up to our behaviour charter in this meeting today?
- What I heard, what I felt, what I think

Or substitute with one of your own. The only guidelines are that:

- Everyone should contribute
- We must speak to the improvement needed, so don't let people get off with saying there isn't anything that could be improved – there always is, and actually, that gives us great data that this might be a team where it isn't okay to learn, show imperfections, question the status quo
- It should be reflective about the work of the team in the meeting
- It shouldn't be about the room, the temperature, or the coffee

A further level of depth can be gained by making this individual reflection about your own or (even deeper) others' performance during the meeting, or you can keep it light by talking about your reflections on the whole group.

Some **questions you might ask** yourself on this element for either your own personal leadership style or that of the leadership team in which you sit include:

- How open are you with your feelings to those around you in your team?
- Do you find it easy to know when to show high levels of vulnerability and when to show clear directive leadership? The most skilled leaders can read a situation and shift gear when needed.
- When was the last time you had a really good personal conversation with your teammates, finding out about their lives, asking them if they are okay, and really waiting to hear and listen to the answer?
- What is your approach to asking for help? Do you find it hard or easy? Who do you ask? Who do you trust to share your need for help with?
- How does this asking for help and admitting mistakes show up in your team? Who does this well and how does that go down with the other members of the team?
- Is your organisation ready for vulnerable leadership? What kinds of role models are in your sector? Can you learn from them?

VULNERABLY
Three Top Tips

Do you like, respect, trust, and care about the people in your team as fellow human beings, as well as co-workers (with reasonable boundaries in place)? Reflect on the trust equation and be curious about whether you display what is required for others to trust you.

YOU

Are people in your team able to ask each other for help when they are struggling or admit a mistake?
Have a conversation with your team about trust, use the trust equation as a starter for the conversation, or add the check-in and check-out to your meetings.

YOUR TEAM

Does your organisation have a learning culture? Is it easy to admit and report errors or near misses? Do people freely ask for help? If not, you might want to find out what stops people and test how psychologically safe people feel in your staff survey, for example.

YOUR ORGANISATION

Figure 48: Vulnerably: Three Top Tips

PART FIVE
AND FINALLY...

What Might You Do Next?

CHAPTER 20

WHAT NEXT?

We hope, as you get to the end of this book, that it has prompted some curiosity within you about how your own leadership and that of the teams you inhabit stack up. We hope you will ask yourself some questions and do something with the information we have provided. Doing something, anything, means you are moving forward and progressing in the never-ending search for improvement as a leader. We are assuming you must have been interested in that improvement to have read the book in the first place!

So, if you are going to do something, anything, what are you going to do?

Having read this book, you might consider evaluating your own leadership maturity and the maturity of your leadership team by testing yourself against elements of the STELLAR MODEL®. You can do that by working through each one separately, using the questions section in each chapter and having a discussion together about how you think you all fare.

Or you can review the whole Maturity Matrix on pages 106 and 107 and see where you think you fair as a team. You can also take the questionnaire as an individual by scanning the QR code on page 108.

However, if there are some issues in the team, maybe it isn't as psychologically safe as you think. Perhaps people aren't too happy sharing their true thoughts yet, so you might get a false positive. This is where you might want to consider bringing in an external person to provide you with the support you need.

CHAPTER 21

CHOOSING YOUR OD OR EXTERNAL SUPPORT PRACTITIONER

Organisational development practitioners can assist organisations with a huge range of change, transformation, improvement, and relational developments across the whole system or between two or more people.

To find the right practitioner to enable your team, organisation, or system to improve can be confusing, especially if the subject matter is not something you are hugely familiar with. It can be a costly and dangerous mistake if you select the wrong person or firm. Therefore, we have put together some tips to help with your selection.

Do you know who you will be working with on your project?

Has the partner of the firm who knows their stuff come to see you to close the deal and win the contract? Will a junior person turn up to deliver your project? This may not, in itself, be an issue, if you know who from the firm is doing what and when, etc. If you aren't getting the big boss on the ground throughout the project, do you have a direct line to them at any time and a weekly checkpoint with them to raise any issues or do you just have a progress check?

What is the experience of the team working in your space?

Are the individuals on your project team believable specialists in the area of skills you need to support your objectives? What are their capabilities and experience? While only very few OD practitioners will be internationally recognised as top writers of business advancement books, there are many credentials, references, qualifications, or experiences that you can check out about the background of the person you might be thinking of working with. You might need to check if individuals from the group have pertinent involvement with your industry or have experience managing your types of concerns or capabilities, for example, if they have a qualification in organisational development. You might want to search recommendations, seek references, etc., but whatever you do, please do some due diligence. Working with an OD practitioner or team coach is as much about chemistry as it is about qualifications and experience. Both are just as important.

How big is the consulting firm?

Organisational development firms are different in size, with some excellent, small, niche companies (present company included!). However, lots of corporate organisations think that "bigger is better".

This isn't generally the truth because an organisational development firm (or the arm of a large consultancy) that appears to have lots of people doesn't always give better help or results.

More significant firms will, in general, have a lot of customers, and your needs may become lost in the mix as they vie for consideration with the requirements of different organisations. Smaller firms can be a superior fit for organisations that need a partner who will focus on their particular needs, as opposed to just applying a standard response to everything.

Make sure you know the answers to these few questions:

- Will they use language that mirrors the terms that the people in your association use?

- Does the content and examples they use mirror the everyday issues lived by your team members?

- Will they flex and customise their models, their slide colours, etc., to co-brand content?

- Would they be able to adjust their approaches to deal with the primary issues that are needed to meet your objectives?

- Does the organisational development firm have an assortment of content and models? Would they be able to furnish specialists with a deep pool of information in your industry or specialists with more extensive experience, as required?

- How flexible is the arrangement that the expert offers?

- Is the fee structure project-based or hourly/per day based, and are you clear about what you are getting for your money?

- Are their approaches based on research and the latest thinking in the field?

This isn't an exhaustive list of questions. There might be many, many more to think about when engaging external advisers in this territory. The most important three considerations are:

- Do you know what you need?

- Do you know what you are buying when you go to market?

- Do you know that what you have bought is the best solution for the issue you have?

If you can't answer these questions yet, then pause and consider if what you need to source right now is some external help to answer these questions!

Get in touch

Clients come to us when they are already performing well together as a team, forming as a new team, welcoming new members to a well-established team, or when the team has or is breaking down and relationships are fractured.

Often, when a new Chief Executive or senior leader joins a team, they will want to "restart" on their terms, with their expectations, and that is a great time to evaluate the current state and set some goals for the future.

Our process involves using the OD cycle, outlined in Chapter 7. In practice, we will have a contracting meeting with the client, agree what is required, then commence the program of data gathering and analysis, arrange the feedback, and plan and deliver an intervention or series of interventions. These are prioritised based on the outcomes of the data gathering analysis and feedback loops. We then work across the client system to deliver positive outcomes, sustainable changes, and a healthy skills transfer and exit or move across the wider system, doing more work.

If you want to know about our work, our clients, or how we can help you improve your leadership or your leadership teams, then get in touch with us via our website https://peopleandodpartners.com/ or email us at admin@peopleandodpartners.com to tell us how you are getting on with the STELLAR MODEL®.

"IT IS AMAZING WHAT YOU CAN ACCOMPLISH IF YOU DO NOT CARE WHO GETS THE CREDIT"

Harry S. Truman

SNEAK PEAK INTO

"LEADING CORPORATE CLANS": A PRACTICIONER'S TOOLKIT

In this second book in the Leading Corporate Clans series, we provide a wide selection of tools, techniques, and exercises with handouts, worksheets, and examples for you to customise or use as is.

Why reinvent the wheel? We want to make it easy for you to run team coaching, workshops and leadership coaching sessions using the STELLAR MODEL® elements and the organisational development cycle.

We will provide a selection of resources to use at each stage of the OD cycle and the outlines of the exercises we use when working with teams, supporting the development of skills in each element of the STELLAR MODEL®. We hope you find them self-explanatory and useful. If you want any more information about how to put them into practice, get in touch.

List of Figures

Reference List

1.   NTL Institute (2022). Organization Development. Available at: https://www.ntl.org/organizational-development/

2.   FLAG Female Leadership and Growth (2022). People and OD Partners. Available at: https://peopleandodpartners.com/what-we-do-1

3.   She Mentors (2022). Mentoring for Purpose-Driven Women. Available at: https://shementors.com.au/

4.   SWS Softwood Self-Publishing (2022). Putting you in control of your publishing journey. Available at: https://www.swspublishing.com/

5.   Mill House Media (2022). Available at: https://millhousemedia.co.uk/

6.   Online as Nullen Art (2022). Available at: https://www.instagram.com/nullenart/?hl=en

7.   Yugambeh Language People (2022). The Yugambeh Museum Language and Heritage Research Centre. Available at: https://www.yugambeh.com/

8.   NTL Institute (2022). Organization Development. Available at: https://www.ntl.org/organizational-development/

9.   Cheung-Judge, M.Y. (2022). NTL Institute Overview. Available at: https://ntl-od.uk/overview

10. Bushe, G. (2022). Gervase Bushe Professional Bio. Available at: http://www.gervasebushe.ca/probio.htm

11. Reddy, W.B. (1994). Intervention Skills: Process Consultation for Small Groups and Teams. San Francisco: Jossey-Bass

12. Lencioni, P. M. (2002). The five dysfunctions of a team. Jossey-Bass.

13. Stavros, J.M. Godwin, L.N. & Cooperrider, D.L. (2015). Organization Development and the Strengths Revolution. In: W.J. Rothwell, J. Stavros, R.L. Sullivan, Practicing Organization Development: Leading Transformation and Change. (4th ed., p. 96). New Jersey: Wiley.

14. Connecting to Excellence (2022). Connecting to Excellence, Team Facilitation and Executive Coaching. Available at https://www.connectingtoexcellence.com/

15. Brown, B. (2018). Dare to lead: Brave work. Tough conversations. Whole hearts. Vermilion.

16. Sinek, S. (2011). Start with why: How great leaders inspire everyone to take action. Penguin Books.

17. Coolangatta (2022). Destination Gold Coast. Available at https://www.destinationgoldcoast.com/places-to-see/coolangatta

18. Huxham, C. (1996). Creating Collaborative Advantage. London: SAGE Publications Ltd.

19. Huxham, C. & Vangen, S. (2009). Doing things collaboratively: realising the advantage or succumbing to inertia? In: Collaborative Governance - A New Era of Public Policy in Australia? The Australian National University, Australia, pp. 29-44.

20. Huxham, C. & Vangen, S. (2009). Doing things collaboratively: realising the advantage or succumbing to inertia? In: Collaborative Governance - A New Era of Public Policy in Australia? The Australian National University, Australia, pp. 29-44.

21. Cummings, T. G. & Worley, C. G. (2015). Organization development and change. Stamford, USA: Cengage Learning.

22. Lewin, K. (1946). Action research and minority problems. Journal of Social Issues. (2) pp.34-46.

23. Clark, P. (1972). Action Research and Organizational Change. Joanna Cotler Books.

24. Davidson, D. (2005). The Organisational Development Cycle: putting the approaches into a process. In E. Peck, Organisational Development in Healthcare: Approaches, Innovations, Achievements. (1st ed., p. 63). Taylor & Francis.

25. Cheung-Judge, M.Y. & Holbeche, L. (2015). Organization Development. A Practitioner's Guide for OD and HR. (2nd ed). Kogan Page: London.

26. Tschudy, T. (2014). An OD Map: The essence of organization development. In B.B. Jones & M. Brazzel, The NTL Handbook of Organization Development and Change. (2nd ed., p.129). San Francisco: Wiley.

27. Jones, B.B. & Brazzel, M. (2014). The NTL Handbook of Organization Development and Change: Principles, Practices, and Perspectives. San Francisco: Pfeiffer.

28.   Noolan, J.A. (2006). Organization Diagnosis Phase. In B.B. Jones & M. Brazzel, The NTL Handbook of Organization Development and Change. (2nd ed., p.192). San Francisco: Pfeiffer.

29.   Hodges, J. (2020). Organization Development: How Organizations Change and Develop Effectively. London: Red Globe Press.

30.   Bushe, G. & Marshak, R.J. (2014). Dialogic Organization Development. In B.B. Jones & M. Brazzel, The NTL Handbook of Organization Development and Change. (2nd ed., p.193). San Francisco: Wiley.

31.   Peck, E. (2005). Organisational Development in Healthcare: Approaches, Innovations, Achievements. Taylor & Francis.

32.   https://en.wikipedia.org/wiki/Myers%E2%80%93Briggs_Type_Indicator

33.   Stirling-Wilkie, G. (2021). From Physical to Virtual Space. How to Design and Host Transformative Spaces Online. British Columbia, Canada:BMI Publishing

34.   Tschudy, T. (2014). An OD Map: The essence of organization development. In B.B. Jones & M. Brazzel, The NTL Handbook of Organization Development and Change. (2nd ed., p.129). San Francisco: Wiley.

35.   Brown, D., Leach, M., & Covey, J. (2005). Organization Development for Social Change. In T.G. Cummings, Handbook of Orgnization Development. Thousand Oaks: SAGE.

36.   Axelrod, D. & Axelrod, E. (2014). Let's Stop Meeting Like This: Tools to Save Time and Get More Done. San Francisco: Berrett-Koehler.

37.   Kirkpatrick, J.D. & Kirkpatrick, W.K. (2016). Kirkpatrick's Four Levels of Training Evaluation. ATD Press.

38.   Weisbord, M. (1985). The organization development contract revisited. Consultation: An international journal, 62 (2), 142-148.

39.   Green B. (2017). Use of the Hippocratic or other professional oaths in UK medical schools in 2017: practice, perception of benefit and principlism. BMC research notes, 10(1), 777. https://doi.org/10.1186/s13104-017-3114-7

40.   Wikipedia. (2022). Prime Directive. Available at: https://en.wikipedia.org/wiki/Prime_Directive

41.   Hackman, R.J. (1990). Work Teams in Organisations: An Orienting Framework, Groups that work (and those that don't). Jossey-Bass

42.   FIRO. (2022). FIRO History and Background. Available at: https://eu.themyersbriggs.com/en/tools/FIRO/FIRO-history

43.   Marshak, R.J. (2006). Covert Processes at Work: Managing the Five Hidden Dimensions of Organizational Change: Managing the Hidden Dimensions of Organizational Change. Berrett-Koehler Publishers.

44.   Gellerman, W., Frankel, M.S., & Ladenson, R.F. (1990). Values and Ethics in Organization and Human Systems Development: Responding to Dilemmas in Professional Life. San Francisco:Jossey-Bass.

45.   Weisbord, M.R. (1987). Productive Workplaces, Organizing and Managing for Dignity, Meaning and Community. San Francisco: Jossey-Bass.

46.   Tolbert, M.A.R. & Hanafin, J. (2006). Use of Self in OD Consulting: What Matters in Presence. Available at: https://maraineyassociates.com/wp-content/uploads/2015/12/UseofSelf-Presence.pdf

47.   Cheung-Judge, M.Y. & Jamieson, D.W. (2022). Global Use of Self Research Report. Available at: https://www.quality-equality.com/uosreport

48.   West, M.A., Borrill, C., Dawson, J., Scully, J., Carter, M., Anelay, S., Patterson, M., & Waring, J. (2002). The link between the management of employees and patient mortality in acute hospitals, The International Journal of Human Resource Management, 13(8), 1299-1310.

49.   Australian Geographic (2022). DNA confirms Aboriginal culture one of Earth's oldest. Available at: https://www.australiangeographic.com.au/news/2011/09/dna-confirms-aboriginal-culture-one-of-earths-oldest/

50.   Wysocki, R.K. (2004). Project Management Process Improvement. London: Artech House.

51.   Katzenbatch, J.R. & Smith, D.K. (1993). The Wisdom of Teams: Creating the High-Performance Organization. McKinsey & Company.

52.   Clutterbuck, D. (2007). Coaching the Team at Work. Nicholas Brearley Publishing.

53.   Myers, G., Cliff, C., & Champoux, T. (2015). Teams that work: The six characteristics of high performing teams. Createspace Independent Publishing Platform.

54. Mindtools. (2022). 5 Whys. Available at: https://www.mindtools.com/pages/article/newTMC_5W. htm#:~:text=The%20method%20is%20remarkably%20simple,prevent%20the%20issue%20from%20 recurring.

55. Sinek, S. (2011). Start with why: How great leaders inspire everyone to take action. Penguin Books.

56. Mindtools. (2022). What Are Your Values? Deciding What's Most Important in Life. Available at: https:// www.mindtools.com/pages/article/newTED_85.htm#:~:text=Deciding%20What's%20Most%20 Important%20in%20Life&text=Your%20values%20are%20the%20things,way%20you%20want%20 it%20to.

57. Brown, B. (2018). Dare to lead: Brave work. Tough conversations. Whole hearts. Vermilion.

58. Delizonna, L. (2017). High-Performing Teams Need Psychological Safety. Here's How to Create It. Available at: https://hbr.org/2017/08/ high-performing-teams-need-psychological-safety-heres-how-to-create-it

59. Clutterbuck, D. (2007). Coaching the Team at Work. Nicholas Brearley Publishing.

60. Kings Fund. (2017). Caring to change. How compassionate leadership can stimulate innovation in health care. Available at: http://www.nhscompassion.org/compassion/wp-content/uploads/2016/02/Caring_ to_change_Kings_Fund_May_2017-1.pdf

61. Marquet, L.D. (2015). Turn The Ship Around! : A True Story of Turning Followers Into Leaders. Penguin Books.

62. Phaal, R. (2022). Sunshine Chart Template. Available at: https://www.cambridgeroadmapping.net/ moretemplates#Link4

63. KISS (2022). Project Management - an overview. Available at: https://expertprogrammanagement. com/2022/02/start-stop-continue/

64. Swanson, D.J. & Creed, A.S. (2014). Sharpening the Focus of Force Field Analysis, Journal of Change Management. 14(1), 28-47, DOI: 10.1080/14697017.2013.788052

65. Jacobs, T., Shepherd, J., & Johnson, G. (1998). Strengths, weaknesses, opportunities and threats (SWOT) analysis. In V. Ambrosini, Exploring Techniques of Analysis and Evaluation in Strategic Management. (p.122). London: Prentice Hall.

66. Task Roll Up - https://peopleandodpartners.com/ resources section

67. Wikipedia (2022). Cartesian coordinate system. Available at:https://en.wikipedia.org/wiki/Cartesian_ coordinate_system#:~:text=A%20Cartesian%20coordinate%20system%20(UK,the%20same%20 unit%20of%20length.

68. Eagles Flight (2022). Want your people to embrace the future? Mindset is Everything. Available at: https://www.eaglesflight.com/asia/

69. Stewart, J. (1984). The Role of Information in Public Accountability. In: A. Hopwood and C. Tomkins, Issues in Public Sector Accounting. (p. 13). Oxford: Philip Allan Publishers Limited.

70. Rosenberg, M. B. (2004). Nonviolent Communication: A Language of Life. (2nd ed). Puddle Dancer Press.

71. Chopra, D. (2014). The Gap. Available at: https://www.deepakchopra.com/articles/the-gap/

72. Dick, B. (2018). 'Turning Points' activity. Available at: http://www.aral.com.au/pdfs/02turningpoints.pdf

www.ingramcontent.com/pod-product-compliance
Lightning Source LLC
Chambersburg PA
CBHW041727210326
41598CB00008B/806